Naturalistic Vivarium Design
Volume I: Desert Vivaria

Philippe de Vosjoli

Advanced Vivarium Systems, Inc.

10728 Propsect Ave., Suite G, Santee, CA 92071

ISBN 1-882770-33-1

PRINTED AND BOUND IN THE UNITED STATES OF AMERICA.

Cover Illustration by Kevin Anderson.
All photography by the author unless indicated.
Graphic Design and Layout by Bridget M. Pilcher and Davina Colvin.
Cover Graphics by Andrew Mansker.

Contents

Introduction 1

General Principles 3

The Vivarium Store 4

Vivarium Terminology 6

Preliminary Considerations 7

The Desert Vivarium 9

An Outline of Steps in Vivarium Design 12

Getting Started 13

Plants for Desert Vivaria 23

Hardware 49

Lighting 50

Heating 52

Vivarium Controls 53

Vivarium Maintenance 55

Animals for Desert Vivaria 56

Keeping Mixed Collections in a Desert Vivarium 58

Vivarium Problems 59

The Vivarium as an Educational Tool 61

Conclusion 62

Useful Information and Sources 63

Introduction

THE AUTHOR WAS first introduced to herpetoculture at the age of twelve, when Monsieur Renaud, an eccentric former keeper at the Jardin des Plantes in Paris, acted as his mentor for a short while. The approach advocated by this man was that of the naturalistic vivarium. To keep and display amphibians and reptiles under simple laboratory-style conditions, he believed, conveyed the wrong impression about these animals, isolating them in human experience from their environment, and preventing them from expressing and demonstrating the range of behavior of which they were capable. Monsieur Renaud thought that beautiful animals had to be kept in beautiful enclosures because, if so, they would affect the human observer much like a great work of art does. As with a hologram, a tiny section of nature, he said, even if simulated in some ways, contained the secrets of the whole, and likewise a well-designed vivarium had the ability to teach about nature, the planet, and human nature. The author, using some of the methods he had been taught, had, by the age of fifteen, already bred several types of amphibians and reptiles.

Keeping amphibians and reptiles in naturalistic vivaria is a radically different approach from keeping them in the near-sterile, laboratory-type captive environments promoted by commercial breeders and most pet stores. The latter approach has been the primary domain of the second wave of herpetoculture, which has focused on commercial captive-breeding. It is space efficient, energy efficient, and, to a degree, labor efficient—at least to set up initially. It is also an approach that distorts the experience of the animals we are keeping and/or selling, placing an unusual emphasis on their production efficiency. In short, it is a technology of amphibian and reptile farming. Unfortunately, second-wave technology has dominated the marketing trends of the pet trade for a long time. Today many of the magical creatures that once made our minds soar have become commercial commodities kept in plastic boxes and sterile enclosures with artificial turf or wood shavings and plastic plants.

The way we keep animals sends a message to others and affects our personal outlook on the world. The greatest problem with the technology of commercial breeding is that it tends to deprive people of the experience of the depth of animals. As a result, we tend to become shallower and less conscious human beings, seeing only the surface of our world. All organisms, and this includes humans, have levels of depth that are greater than at first meets the eye. They have a depth of structure that, in the case of amphibians and reptiles, can be revealed through herpetology: the study of the biology of amphibians and reptiles. They also have evolutionary and ecological depth which is revealed through the study of paleontology, anatomy, and ecology. There are only two ways that we can gain insights into the latter level of depth in amphibians and reptiles: either to observe and study the animals in their natural habitat or to observe and study them in naturalistic vivaria which strive to simulate some of the essential elements of their natural habitat. Organisms also have mental depth, an experience of reality that is uniquely their own. The study of animal behavior and empathy are the vehicles by which we can understand this last level of depth.

The third-wave approach to keeping amphibians and reptiles is a systems-oriented technology that places an emphasis on naturalistic vivarium design. The goal is to provide animals with more complex and more stimulating environments that simulate some, and we hope many, of the essential elements of their natural habitats. The focus of keeping amphibians and reptiles thus becomes re-creating parts of their world in our homes. These creations, as we will see, can be beautiful, they can move us, and they can affect our views of the world. In the long run we will all gain by shifting to a third-wave approach to keeping amphibians and reptiles. We will experience our animals in a new light and ideally learn from them. The animals will have an opportunity to do more of what they are neurologically wired to do and possibly lead happier lives. People involved in the pet industry will have opportunities to generate more business.

This book presents basic principles of desert vivarium design that I have developed over the past twenty years. I consider them as baby steps into a field we are just beginning to explore. The potential of naturalistic vivaria is so great that it could significantly affect what most humans know about the world. They can be a doorway whereby we are allowing nature to enter our homes and our minds.

A 36-inch long vivarium, designed for keeping frog-eyed geckos (Teratoscincus kyserlingii) and Jone's armadillo lizards (Cordylus jonesi). The frog-eyed geckos in this picture although thin, were first quarantined and deparasitized. They have fared well in this particular vivarium.

General Principles

WHAT THIS BOOK is about: This is the first popular book that deals specifically and exclusively with the design of naturalistic desert vivaria for the keeping of reptiles. Unlike many other books in the trade—which avoid the details of designing a vivarium and provide only generalized information on supplies, plants, and putting together of a vivarium—this book is a detailed how-to book that takes you through the actual process of design from planning to completion.

What this book is not about: This book provides no information on the keeping of amphibians or reptiles, other than listing several species that will fare well in these naturalistic enclosures. The details of care, maintenance, and breeding of these various species can be found in other books specializing in such subjects.

An Outlook on Vivarium Design

Once caught up in the vivarium-centered approach to herpetoculture, a reptile or amphibian owner's outlook broadens and he or she undergoes a philosophical, as well as a conceptual, transformation toward animal keeping. The old goal may have been simply to keep animals; the new goal becomes to create a complex set of interrelationships that includes the environment, the animals, and the effect of the whole on the human observer.

The end result is an artistic and dynamic creation. When well designed, each component in a vivarium becomes part of a work of art, from the rocks and woods selected to the plants, the animals, and the final overall design. This kind of vivarium eventually affects the way you think about amphibians and reptiles. You will go to a store and select animals not only by their appearance, but also in accordance with the potential environment you can design for them. It is not really possible to convey the excitement and involvement that you can enjoy with a well-designed vivarium. You cannot truly know about this until you experience it. The creative outlet of the vivarium adds elements that make herpetoculture even more fascinating than it was before this new trend emerged in the United States. The impact of this new phase will be tremendous, comparable to what has happened in the marine aquarium hobby with the advent of the mini-reef system.

A desert vivarium on display at a major pet trade show.

The Vivarium Store

At the time of this writing, there are no vivarium stores in the United States. In the late 1970s there existed one naturalistic vivarium store in New York City called Small Worlds, which had a high degree of popularity and success until its closing. The naturalistic vivarium concept has yet to permeate the general pet trade. A vivarium store is not just a store that sells amphibians and reptiles; it is primarily a store that sells environments, environmental concepts, and environmental supplies for the keeping of amphibians, reptiles, and select invertebrates.

The vivarium is to herpetoculture what the mini-reef system has been to the keeping of saltwater fish. It is revolutionary and carries considerable economic implications. As with mini-reef systems, the key to designing a successful vivarium store is to have samples of vivaria on display, and some of the amphibians and reptiles for sale should be displayed in naturalistic vivaria. The next step is to have supplies on hand, which means having enclosures, substrata, plants, rocks, woods, lighting, heating, watering systems and pumps, thermostats, timers, thermometers, and so on. Well-designed vivaria are works of art that fascinate and move people who observe them. In Europe, a naturalistic vivarium is commonly the centerpiece of a living room or family room.

Advantages of a Specialized Vivarium Store

Principal advantages of a specialized vivarium store are saving time and money, and preventing frustration. This refers to a hypothetical future in which vivarium stores will exist; currently, U.S. herpetoculture seems stuck in the narrow-sighted second wave of herpetoculture: captive breeding. But, once customers become acquainted with the delightful potential of a naturalistic vivarium in their home, the demand for the necessary supplies with which to create these enclosures will call forth a shift in priorities. When the first vivarium stores become established, the consumer will find numerous advantages that will greatly facilitate vivarium design. At the time of this writing, however, finding the supplies to assemble a naturalistic vivarium is a time-consuming and sometimes frustrating experience. Finding rocks, wood, substrates, and plants may mean numerous phone inquiries, many trips, and hours of time investigating; finding the right lights, heating and monitoring equipment could take at least as long. Many times the author has found that the greatest frustration to be the time needed to locate the basic supplies required for assembling a vivarium. It has taken a day or more simply to find nurseries that offer an interesting selection of plants. Consumers who found what they were looking for in specialized vivarium stores would gladly pay a little extra for the items they seek in exchange for the time they would save.

Requirements for a Vivarium Store

1. A room specifically dedicated to naturalistic vivaria
2. Prototype vivaria on permanent display
   - Desert vivarium
   - Tropical forest vivarium
   - Shallow depth shoreline vivarium with miniature waterfall
   - Greater depth shoreline vivarium
3. Supplies
   - Enclosures including front-opening vivaria
   - Stands for enclosures
   - Substrates including
     pea gravel
     potting soils for tropical plants and succulents
     plants
     sand, different types and sizes
     orchid bark
     dried green moss
   - Landscape materials
     rocks
     woods, including grapewood and cholla
     freshwater driftwood
     tree stumps and roots
     cork bark, flats and rounds

Live-plant display units should include a wide selection of plants for desert, tropical, and shoreline vivaria. (Great emphasis should be placed on the availability of a wide selection of plants. Without live plants, you do *not* have a naturalistic vivarium store.)

   - Lighting fixtures
     fluorescent-type fixtures
     incandescent reflector-type fixtures
   - Light bulbs
     regular incandescent bulbs
     incandescent spotlights
     red incandescent bulbs
     fluorescent full-spectrum bulbs
     BL-type black lights
     other improved bulbs as they appear on the market
   - Heating supplies
     subtank heaters
     submersible heaters
     ceramic infrared bulbs
   - Control and monitoring equipment
     thermometers
     thermostats
     rheostats
     timers
     pH test kits
     ammonia and nitrite test kits
     water hardness test kits
   - Miniature fans, such as those used to cool electronic equipment
   - Water pumps and supplies for miniature waterfalls
4. A selection of animals suitable for naturalistic vivaria.
5. Trained personnel. (Employees *must* know principles of vivarium design. This cannot be overemphasized; knowledgeable employees help generate sales and repeat sales, and over time bring in new customers.)

Vivarium Terminology

VIVARIUM: A PLACE, usually an indoor glass-fronted or glass-sided enclosure, for the keeping of animals and/or plants under conditions that simulate some of the essential elements of an animal or plant habitat; a term currently used primarily in conjunction with the keeping of amphibians and reptiles, it can also include certain insects and arachnids, such as theraphosid spiders (tarantulas)

Naturalistic vivarium: A vivarium designed to imitate, or give the appearance of nature.

Vivarist: An individual involved in the art and science of keeping animals and plants in vivaria.

Topography of a vivarium: The surface features of the inside of the vivarium, including landscaping features.

Topographical stratification: Creating layers in the topography of a vivarium; the process of creating layers in the topography of a vivarium.

To stratify the space of a vivarium: To create layers in the space of a vivarium through topographical stratification.

Niche: The particular area within a habitat occupied by an organism.

Vivarium niche: Areas within the vivarium designed to cater to the environmental needs of a particular species.

A 24-inch long vivarium designed for keeping microgeckos (Tropiocolotes). Notice the stratified topography. The small Sansevieria in this vivarium is Bally #12681, a small, short, fat-stemmed, branching species (middle left). In the back is a Sansevieria canaliculata dwarf from Madagascar, with thin vertical cylindrical leaves. In the front are various Haworthias and a small Euphorbia milli roseana (in bloom). The vivarium is heated with a subtank heat pad on a rheostat and lit by four two-foot fluorescent full-spectrum bulbs.

Preliminary Considerations

Designing a naturalistic vivarium requires planning and forethought. Haphazard assembly is unwise; it is time consuming and expensive (the cost of correcting mistakes), and it often leads to frustration and disappointment in the end. Thus, take the time to plan and visualize the kind of vivarium you would like to create. Think of placement, size, types of plants and animals—the works. The following are general guidelines that will help you formulate your initial design plans.

1. Selection of animals. Avoid very large reptiles. They crush, scratch, tear, and dig up plants as well as landscape structures. Because of their size and appetite, large reptiles also produce large feces, which require frequent cleaning of a vivarium and replacement of substrate. Large reptiles can be kept in naturalistic vivaria only if you are willing to allocate a room or a large part of a room for their maintenance.

2. Size of the enclosure(s). As a rule of thumb when designing naturalistic vivaria, the length of a vivarium should be a minimum of 20 inches and at least five times the total length of the largest reptile or amphibian housed therein. The width should be a minimum of 10 inches and at least one-and-a-half times the length of the largest reptile or amphibian. For snakes, apply a formula whereby the vivarium will be a length one-and-a-half times the length of the longest snake, and a width at least half the length of the longest snake. (These recommendations are in sharp contrast to minimum recommendations for maintenance in captivity, which are typically an enclosure having a perimeter at least one-and-a-half times the length of the snake species maintained.)

3. Density of animals. All naturalistic vivaria work best with relatively few animals. A general measure of appropriate density for naturalistic vivaria is that the sum of the total lengths of animals in the vivarium should not exceed three-fourths the length of the vivarium. For snakes, the total length(s) of the animal(s) should not exceed the length of the vivarium.

For example: in a four-foot-long vivarium you could keep two collared lizards and a pair of small armadillo lizards, or a trio of ornate *Uromastyx*, or five leopard geckos. Some people may think this is quite a low density, but keeping plants and animals together is a different approach, espoused by a *very* different philosophy of animal keeping from that used by commercial breeders. The philosophy of naturalistic vivarium design is to minimize maintenance, and that is possible only with low densities of animals. When combined with plants, these densities will be more than enough to create an aesthetic display.

If you have a community vivarium in which several species cohabit and dwell in different vivarium niches, then you can increase the densities so that the sum of the total lengths of the reptiles equals the total length of the vivarium.

Some Useful References

Your best inspiration for vivarium design will always come from direct observation of the animal species you are keeping in their natural habitats. Serious vivarists will travel to study the species they are keeping and to get a sense of the optimal conditions for keeping and breeding them in captivity.

A camera is an essential tool during these expeditions. So are thermometers, including digital thermometers with probes (which can be dropped into burrows or placed inside shelters), and digital hygrometers to determine relative humidity, as well as light meters to measure light intensity. Unfortunately, many of us are too busy or lack the finances to undertake such expeditions and therefore must rely on information conveyed by knowledgeable people and by reference books.

There are currently a number of good books available on the herpetoculture of various species, books that will inform you of the maintenance requirements and, in some cases, of design possibilities for naturalistic vivaria for particular species. When you can find them, some of the best references are herpetological works that describe or show photographs of a species' habitat. Some of these references can be found in university libraries and can be bought from book dealers who advertise in various herpetological newsletters and publications. If possible, research the library at a university with a good herpetological reference library. The first step is to look in the book collection by searching the library catalog by subject. The next step is to look for articles in scientific or other types of publications. The easiest way to find herpetological articles pertaining to your species is to consult the Zoological Record, going back at least 20 years. Ask a librarian for help on how to use the Zoological Record.

Ask for book recommendations from someone already keeping the species you intend to keep. The best person to ask may not necessarily be the pet shop owner, because many of them have very little experience in the keeping of the animals they sell, and they may not have read the books. Get the best information available; it could mean the difference between success and failure for your vivarium project, between life and death for your animals.

If you cannot find useful information, which unfortunately is often the case, you will have to plan a vivarium design to offer enough topographical diversity that the animals you are keeping have their needs met, and in so doing, provide you with essential information.

To help with the aesthetics of the vivarium and the positioning of plants, you may find that travel books, geography books, and books on gardening will prove useful. Books with photographs of desert areas can give you a sense of how real deserts and semiarid areas look. Books on rock-garden designs, including Zen rock gardens, will prove very useful in helping you acquire a sense of how to balance various elements in the design of a vivarium. Many public libraries have good reference sections on nature and gardening, making these kinds of books readily available to everyone. If you want to acquire a reference library, many of the larger bookstores—and some bookstores specializing in works on horticulture and gardening—have books that you may find useful and inspiring.

Sandfish (Scincus scincus) are now imported with some regularity from Egypt. They will thrive in desert vivaria with a sand substrate. Other lizards in the same size range such as small lacertids or climbing geckos can be kept in the same vivarium.
Photo by Bill Love.

The Desert Vivarium

ALTHOUGH YOU MIGHT think that the name suggests otherwise, a desert vivarium aims to simulate the essential elements of a broad range of arid and semiarid habitats. It is suitable for a variety of species that inhabit a variety of areas. These may include dry ground surface, scrub, rocky or sandy habitats, and dry tropical forests. Note that vivarists do not usually attempt to duplicate or reproduce a natural habitat exactly. It is not practical to do so with many arid and semiarid habitats, in which native and habitat-specific plants usually are difficult, if not impossible, to establish under vivarium conditions. As a general rule, reptile species that can tolerate low to moderate relative humidity will fare well in desert vivaria. The term *desert vivarium* is thus a somewhat arbitrary term used to define a type of vivarium with: (1) relatively dry substrate, (2) rock-based or dry-wood landscaping, (3) low to moderate relative humidity, (4) succulent or arid-climate plants, and (5) high daytime heat and light levels—rather than a vivarium that simulates a specific habitat.

Selection of Enclosures

Because there will be several inches of substrata in a naturalistic vivarium and sizable landscape features, including rocks and plants, you should use at least standard-size enclosures. Do not use low enclosures such as 15-gallon vivaria, which have the same length and width measurements as a standard 20-gallon enclosure but less height. The only advantage of low enclosures with desert vivaria is that it will be less difficult to achieve the high light levels required by many desert plants and the high heat levels required by many diurnal desert animals.

However, this applies only when you are *not* designing a naturalistic desert vivarium. By the time you add substrates and landscape structures, you lose at least three-to-four inches of height. Taller enclosures also will allow you to use taller plants, such as small trees and/or shrubs, to increase vertical stratification and to build the rock work that is desirable for many saxicolous (rock-dwelling) species. Plants in tall desert vivaria have to be selected and positioned carefully in relation to lights. Plants requiring high light will have to be placed within reach of the top of the vivarium, and small spotlights may be necessary to provide additional light for these species.

Wider enclosures will allow for greater topographical stratification of the vivarium space. They also allow you to create designs of greater visual interest.

Commercial Enclosures

There are now readily available several brands of inexpensive vivaria with sliding-screen tops, which can work well for desert vivaria. Their primary flaw is their relatively thin glass, which could cause problems if you use much rock work or heavy substrate in the vivarium. Another flaw is the sliding-screen tops; if the vivarium is placed against a wall, the sliding top must slide away from the wall, thereby making your access to the vivarium difficult. If the top is to slide toward the wall, the vivarium must be placed at a distance equal to its width from the wall, which is less attractive, somewhat awkward, and an ineffective use of space; also, any lights above the screen top must be moved whenever the enclosure is opened.

The author's favorite enclosures are the high-quality, all-glass vivarium enclosures with sliding-glass fronts and heavy-duty screen, manufactured by Vivarium Research

Group, Inc. Sliding-glass fronts facilitate designing, landscaping, and maintenance of naturalistic vivaria. A potential problem with these enclosures is their front opening, through which lizards and other animals could escape, but they typically move toward the back, away from the human observer. Neodesha Plastics® currently markets a line of enclosures that sport a space age design, with sliding-glass fronts and molded plastic sides.

Custom-made Enclosures

You can order custom-made enclosures from various companies and individuals. Some of these enclosures are made of glass, some are made of glass and wood, and others are made of melamine-coated pressboard and glass. If you use wood or melamine-coated wood, you should line the bottom with a plastic liner, such as those sold for creating outdoor pools, or with a plastic tub. Plants and watering should be limited to the floor space covered by the tub. If you use marine plywood, you can coat the inside of the vivarium with several layers of marine epoxy paint. You can convert fiberglass or plastic bath and shower stalls, as well as jacuzzi tubs, into desert vivaria.

Custom-made enclosures can be constructed from a variety of materials; photographs of a number of examples are presented in this book. It is *essential* to remember that the material used to build the bottom of the enclosure must withstand long-term exposure to water or a wet medium; plexiglass or glass bottoms are ideal materials for this purpose. You can have glass or plexiglass cut to fit and place it inside the bottoms of various enclosures. If you use wood, you can seal it by using several coats of a marine-grade epoxy paint.

Vivarium Stands

Once in place, a vivarium will not be moveable. Most people elect to place their vivaria on a commercially built aquarium stand or on a custom-built stand, which you can special-order from a cabinet maker. The vivarium stand is an integral component of the aesthetics of a vivarium, and if possible, you should acquire a stand that blends with the decor of the room in which you place the vivarium. In the authors' experience, most aquarium stands are not tall enough for people to view aquaria or vivaria comfortably. The height of a stand should be at least three feet to allow for proper viewing. With tall vivaria that can open only from the top, you may need a small ladder or foot stool in order to perform some aspects of maintenance.

Note: be especially careful when setting a vivarium on a piece of existing furniture. The furniture piece must be capable of bearing the weight of the completed vivarium, and its surface must be level. Any glass tank may develop pressure cracks if it is set on an uneven surface. You should also realize that the piece of furniture used as a vivarium stand could be damaged by scratches, weight impressions, or water stains.

Making a Plan

It is important that you make a plan on paper before setting out to purchase supplies for a desert vivarium. Draw the following: the enclosure according to scale, as seen from the front, and on another sheet of paper; the enclosure as seen from the top. Draw in the substrate layers. Next, sketch in a background, followed by stratification layers, and finally basking rocks and shelters. Then add plants to the drawing. Do this for both front and overhead perspectives of the enclosure. Use a pencil with an eraser so that you can make changes easily. Later, when you go out to select rocks, plants, and woods, you will find these plans invaluable in helping you make your choices. The entire process will be easier, as well as more effective and more likely to work. Remember: ultimately, the vivarium is a work of art and the outcome of a creative process. Making a sketch of your plan will facilitate the final laying down of the vivarium components. After you have made a plan, you should compile a list of the supplies required for you to create your desert vivarium.

For a front-opening desert vivarium, 50 inches by 18 inches, for example, your list might include the following items:

- ❏ Stand (special order from a local aquarium store)
- ❏ Granitic sand: 75 pounds
- ❏ Rocks: two flat, three rounded (one with a flat top, two small); reddish limestone or natural marble
- ❏ Wood: grape? ironwood? root buttress?
- ❏ Cork bark sections and/or cork tube
- ❏ Plants: three or four Sansevierias, one or two Aloe or Gasteria plants, and possibly an elephant *(Bursera)* tree
- ❏ Food-storage containers into which plants can be transferred
- ❏ Tropic Zone® or Flex Watt® heat strip
- ❏ One rheostat
- ❏ One pulse-proportional thermostat
- ❏ One four-foot two-bulb fluorescent fixture
- ❏ One two-foot two-bulb fluorescent fixture
- ❏ One large spotlight reflector/fixture
- ❏ One small spotlight reflector/fixture
- ❏ ZooMed's® Reptisun™ UVB310 lamps
- ❏ One BL-type blacklight bulb
- ❏ One 120-watt spotlight bulb
- ❏ One 100-watt spotlight bulb
- ❏ One surge suppressor/multi-outlet
- ❏ One appliance three-prong timer

Vivarium Topographical Considerations

You should plan your vivarium carefully before putting the design in place. You must give important consideration to how the landscape structures affect the topography of your vivarium and how this in turn affects the space available to the animals you plan to maintain. If the animals are primarily fossorial or terrestrial dwelling, either in the ground or active primarily on the surface of the ground, then taking up a lot of space with rock work will seriously reduce their activity area, quite possibly to their detriment.

On the other hand, if the animals are primarily active on rocks, then stratifying the space with rock work will increase their activity areas. Thus, the key question should be, "How would this topographical element affect the activity areas of the type(s) of animal(s) that I intend to keep?" If the animals are terrestrial and active primarily on flat ground, you will not be able to create a topographically diverse vivarium—unless you have a very large enclosure or a very small species.

Drawing out a plan will help you see how landscape structures affect activity areas. For example, if you choose a terrarium enclosure with a built-in plastic background, one-third of the enclosure surface area will be taken up by the background. By the time you add plants and/or rocks, less than 50 percent of the ground surface will remain available to your animals. And the plastic backgrounds provide so few irregularities of surface that most rock-dwelling lizards cannot use them effectively.

Time Required to Set Up a Naturalistic Vivarium

Once you have successfully assembled all the necessary equipment and supplies, you can assemble a standard 48-inch (1.2-m) vivarium into an impressive showpiece in an afternoon or an evening (two to three hours). Obtaining the supplies, however, can require from one to two days if materials can be found locally, or two to three weeks if they must be mail-ordered. In the author's experience, even if all supplies are available within a 20-mile radius, it could still require a day or more to obtain all the necessary supplies. Let's hope that fully equipped reptile stores offering a wide variety of vivarium supplies will be established in the not-too-distant future.

An Outline of Steps in Vivarium Design

THERE IS A general order in which a desert vivarium is designed. The following list indicates some of the various options.

1. Decide where in a room you will place your vivarium. As a rule, an area that receives only indirect or filtered light from a window will be suitable. Do not place a vivarium (particularly an all-glass vivarium) in front of a window that receives direct sunlight, because of the risk of overheating the plants and animals. Of course the location should be one that would be aesthetically pleasing in terms of room design and furnishings. After you select the location, put in place—and be sure to level—a suitable stand on which to set the vivarium enclosure.

2. Install the subtank heating mat or strip, if you choose to use one. (It is generally recommended.) Place the enclosure on the stand.

3. Add a thin layer of substrate or the drainage layer.

4. Arrange the main landscape structures, such as any background you wish to use and any large rocks.

5. Put in place additional landscape structures such as smaller rocks.

6. Add the growing medium, or place plants in pots.

7. Place the plants in the growing medium, either directly or in plant pipes [see section on Plants].

8. Add any extra rocks or landscape materials.

9. Adjust plants in the landscape so that it looks aesthetically pleasing and fits your design goals.

10. Add lights and additional heat systems, if these are appropriate.

11. Add appropriate timers, thermostats, and thermometers.

12. Make adjustments.

Note: Some people choose to wait a day or two before introducing the animals into their newly created environment. This allows time for last-minute rearranging of small details without disturbing, unsettling, and unduly stressing animals immediately following their relocation.

Spiny-tailed monitor (Varanus acanthurus). These small and attractive monitors are now captive-bred in small numbers and are ideal for a desert vivarium. Photo by Bill Love.

Getting Started

Before getting started you need to decide whether you want to resort to a modular "sunken-plant-pot" approach to vivarium design or an ecologically more complex naturalistic vivarium "plant-in-substrate" approach. Each method has its challenges, its pros and cons.

Sunken-pot Approach

The sunken-pot approach uses a uniform, easily replaceable substrate, into which live plants are placed in pots. This is the preferred method of many vivarists. You also have the option of eliminating live plants entirely, simply using rocks, dry woods, and other dry plant material to design an attractive vivarium. This approach is generally more desirable when housing larger species, as they tend to damage live plants unless their enclosures are very large.

The most commonly used approach is to use a single substrate, either a sand or a pea gravel, and to bury the pots or containers holding the plants in the substrate. The advantages are: (1) the animals cannot readily dig up the plants; (2) watering the plants will mean watering only the soil in the pots rather than the entire substrate; (3) moisture will be contained and evaporate less quickly, and; (4) the plants can easily be removed and replaced as needed. Illustration by Kevin Anderson.

Substrates for the submerged-pot approach

When using the sunken-pot approach, most herpetoculturists use only one kind of substrate. As a rule, at least three inches of substrate (approximately 1 1/2 to 2 pounds per gallon of vivarium volume) will be required. The following are some recommended substrates.

Sand

Selecting a sand for desert vivaria can be difficult. Different grades and types of sand have different properties.

Sand with rounded, variable-size grains

This type of sand is sometimes available in Southern California. The grains vary in color and size but are generally quite rounded. This type of sand has a clean, appealing look. Heat flows through it better than it does through silica sand, although not as well as through pea gravel. The sand found at the edges of certain ant nests is somewhat coarser—but with similar qualities—and is sought out by herpetoculturists seriously involved in vivarium design. Other sand that functions well in desert vivaria are decomposed granite sand and oolithic sand. Fine, smooth-grained black beach sand is available in some areas; it can be very attractive when used with the right combination of rocks and animals.

Silica sand

Fine silica sand (# 30) is used by many herpetoculturists for keeping desert lizards. Although it works for many species, it has certain flaws. For one thing, it is too dense to allow much subtank heat to reach the surface; coarser sand that allows for more air to flow between the particles is easier to heat efficiently. Another flaw is that any kind of moisture will cause fine silica sand particles to stick together. When this sand is wet, it will stick to animals' bodies, including their eyes. If animals dig, dried fine silica sand generates quite a bit of dust. Silica sand also is awkward aesthetically. With several species of desert reptiles it doesn't look or feel quite right; it appears unnatural—too even, too perfect.

Fine pea gravel

After it is washed, pea gravel generates little dust. When it is wet, it usually doesn't stick to animals as readily as sand; many herpetoculturists prefer this type of substrate. Subtank heat rises more readily through pea gravel than it does through sand. Taking the time to select a pea gravel that looks natural and that is relatively uniform in color will make for a more appealing vivarium.

Ingestion of Harmful Substrate Materials

One of the problems with keeping desert reptiles in naturalistic vivaria is the potentially harmful effect of substrate materials, especially if they are ingested by the animals. Of particular concern is silica sand, which in certain small specimens of reptiles can abrade the lining of the gastrointestinal (GI) tract if this sand is ingested too frequently. In some other species, ingested sand may remain lodged in the GI tract. This is of greatest concern with vegetarian reptiles such as chuckwallas, uromastyx, and tortoises. Possibly because of the structure of their GI tract (including a multilobed or multichambered stomach and a long intestine), problems of gastrointestinal impaction from ingested substrate are not uncommon in these vegetarian reptiles.

With these animals it is highly recommended that you select substrate material coarse enough that it cannot be ingested, or use feeding procedures that prevent the ingestion of substrate material.

Desert reptiles that are primarily vegetarian are commonly compulsive diggers and consequently may pile substrate on their food when it is offered in very shallow dishes. Never offer plant matter directly on the substrate when feeding vegetarian reptiles. The author has had autopsies performed on young uromastyx of two species that showed the probable cause of death as substrate impaction of the GI tract. In another instance, a pancake tortoise, captive-raised from a hatchling on a sand substrate, died of gastrointestinal impaction.

With insectivorous species substrate impaction rarely occurs. However, you still should monitor these lizards in order to assure that the selection of substrate material doesn't lead to a high incidence of ingestion. Several species of desert geckos, such as frog-eyed geckos (*Teratoscincus*) and leopard geckos (*Eublepharis macularius*), commonly ingest sand; in the wild this may serve as a source of calcium and is normal behavior for these species. Use a sand containing some limestone, which is preferable to a silica sand for these lizards. Observe your animals, and read up on their habits to determine the best substrate material for their maintenance.

Sunken-Pipe Approach

An alternative to the sunken-pot approach is to transfer plants to sections of large PVC pipes which are partially buried in substrate or placed over a drainage layer. Potting soil is added to the pipe sections and plants transferred from pot to pipe. The advantage is that water will stay relatively contained as plants can be individually watered. The roots of the plants can grow into the moist areas of the drainage layer. A surface layer of substrate is added to just cover the pipe sections. Plant removal and replacement is easy with this system.

An alternative is to use a three-level substrate consisting of a drainage layer, a layer of growing medium, and a surface layer such as sand or pea gravel. The plants are removed from their pots and placed in vertical sections of PVC pipe placed just above the drainage layer or a layer of growing medium. The pipes and plants are put in place right after the growing medium is poured. The surface substrate is applied last, to a level flush with the base of the plants. The pipes allow for individual plant watering; enough moisture seeps through the pipe for the plants to form roots in the growing medium or drainage layer. As a result, plants tend to grow larger. This works very well with small to medium animals.
Illustration by Kevin Anderson.

Complex-Naturalistic Vivarium Approach

The other approach to designing a desert vivarium uses a three- or four-layered substrate, into which plants are planted directly. With this approach the plants will put out roots running throughout the vivarium, and thus you create a miniature ecosystem. The great advantage to this system is that you eventually create a type of ecosystem wherein animal-plant-soil interactions will be similar to those found in the wild; however, watering can also become a problem, precisely because the roots run throughout the substrate. Plants may also grow too large or become invasive with this type of system. If a plant does not fare well and needs to be removed, the entire landscape ultimately may have to be redone.

Because the complex approach uses live plants growing directly in the substratum, it is recommended that you use a three- or four-layered substratum. At the bottom of the vivarium there should be a drainage layer, consisting of 1 to 1 1/2-inches of coarse pebbles or pea gravel. Above that, place a 1/4-inch layer of fine gravel such as #3 aquarium gravel. An alternative is to place plastic mesh or screening over that layer. The purpose of these thin layers is to create a barrier that prevents the growing medium from sifting through into the drainage layer. When you use screening, you should monitor the vivarium to be sure that burrowing animals do not dig under the screening and get stuck there. Above the fine gravel or screening layer, you

Surface layer →
Growing medium →
Screen or fine substrate →
Drainage layer →

Another method uses the same substrate layers as above, but the plants are placed directly in the growing medium. In time a small ecosystem will be formed as some waste matter in the upper substrates will dissolve and reach the bottom layers. This works best with smaller animals but also works with medium-size non-digging species. Illustration by Kevin Anderson.

Step by Step Vivarium Design

The all-glass enclosure should be placed on a stand that makes viewing easy. The next step is to place a subtank heater between the bottom of the enclosure and the stand. Follow instructions carefully. The temperature of the subtank heater should be controlled by a rheostat or a thermostat.

As an alternative to using a thick drainage layer of substrate, undergravel filter plates are placed at the bottom of the enclosure.

A layer of pebble substrate is placed on top of the filter plates. Then a section of grape wood with good character is positioned in the set-up as a vivarium centerpiece.

For growing plants, the drain pipe systems is selected. Sections of large diameter PVC pipes are partially buried in the pebble substrate.

Plants are added including geraniums (left and center), a pony-tailed palm (Beaucarnea recurvata) and a small species of spineless Opuntia. Additional substrate material was added as well as a rock and another section of wood.

should place a 1 1/2- to 2-inch layer of slightly moistened, sandy, peat-based soil mixture (with 30 percent coarse sand). You should then remove the plants from their pots and plant them directly in the mix. Next, add a one-inch layer of sand or pea gravel to form the upper surface level of substrate.

An Overview of Substrates for Complex Naturalistic Vivaria

The drainage layer

The drainage layer is a critical component of successful desert vivaria. It is the first substrate layer you will place in a vivarium and should consist of at least 1 1/2 inches of a medium-grade crushed rock, preferably a porous rock such as the crushed coral rock sold for setting up marine aquaria. The best choice is the white pumice sold by nurseries specializing in cacti and succulents, but this is generally difficult to find. Crushed lava rock, sold in some fish stores or in plant nurseries for landscaping, will also work.

The idea is to use, whenever possible, a porous rock, which will absorb some of the excess water that may filter down into this layer. Pebbles or a coarse aquarium gravel will work, but none of the water will be absorbed; consequently, a layer of water will accumulate in the drainage layer, increasing the risk of rotting the roots of plants that have penetrated this layer. An expensive alternative is to substitute the fired clay pellets used in hydroponic gardening. To estimate the amount of drainage substrate required, estimate roughly a pound of drainage substrate per gallon; thus a three-foot-long 40-gallon vivarium would require about 40 pounds of gravel as a drainage layer.

An alternative approach increasingly used by herpetoculturists is to place undergravel filter plates as a substitute for the drainage layer. Placing a thin layer of pea gravel over the plates is recommended, to prevent the plate slits from clogging up.

The growing medium

The growing medium is the second layer you should use in naturalistic desert vivaria.

As a rule, you should not use commercially sold cactus potting mixes unless you have the opportunity to inspect them. Any mixtures that appear coarse and flaky and that contain white pumice are good choices. Poor choices are mixes that are simply potting soil with some sand mixed in. They lack the drainage and aeration required for plants in desert vivaria. One recommended alternative is to use a high-quality potting mix—without perlite, which tends to rise to the surface when watered and may be ingested by the animals—and mix in up to 50 percent of either pumice, crushed coral, or a crushed limestone gravel. This layer should be at least two inches deep. If you can't find these materials, use a coarse aquarium sand or a fine-grade coarse pebble. Some vivarists add a certain percentage of fine-grade orchid bark, about ten percent, to replace the coarse substrate component. The mix you choose should be determined by the plants you select for the vivarium. Plants from very arid locales will require a very well-drained, airy mix.

The surface medium

After you have added plants and last-minute landscape structures, add the surface medium to the vivarium. This can be a coarse sand, a fine-to-medium-grade pea gravel, or a mixed medium consisting of fine sands in some areas and fine gravel and/or crushed rock in other areas. If you live in a desert region, some of the coarse sands found around the openings of certain ant nests are a good choice.

Finding substrates

Until substrates specifically selected and formulated for vivaria become commercially available, you will have to search for sources. The author recommends using the Yellow Pages of your telephone directory to make inquiries from tropical fish stores, plant nurseries, and suppliers of rocks, gravel, and sand for landscaping purposes. If you live near a desert or in semiarid areas, you can gather suitable substrates from nature. Always take care when gathering substrates or landscape materials from nature. First, make sure that you have permission to collect materials from a particular area, and second, do so with care, being especially sure not to damage or alter the environment.

Basic Principles of Vivarium Landscaping

As was mentioned earlier, the design of a vivarium requires a careful balance that fulfills the needs of the animals and plants placed within it, while being aesthetically pleasing to the human observer. How visually interesting the topography of a vivarium will be in terms of design and composition will be determined by the choice of landscape materials, of both nonliving (rocks, dried wood, manmade materials) and living (plants). Nonetheless, the basic design requirements are focused on the needs of the animals (the most directly affected higher life-forms in the enclosure). For keeping desert reptiles these basic design considerations are listed below.

1. Activity areas. Any desert animal has a preferred activity area. If an animal is primarily active on the surface of the ground, you will need to incorporate large areas of open surface into the landscape design. If an animal primarily dwells among rocks, you will need to include large areas of rock in the vivarium. If the animal is fossorial (burrowing), you will need to provide large areas of burrowing substrate. In the case of rock-dwelling or tree-climbing animals, activity areas can be increased by stratifying the landscape, adding and layering rock or wood in the vivarium. Space can be stratified horizontally or vertically, depending on the needs of the animals.

2. Basking areas. Basking areas typically consist of rock or wood, either a single piece or a stack that will allow animals to thermoregulate in relation to an overhead heat source. You should incorporate at least one basking area in the design of vivaria for active diurnal desert lizards, or preferably, two. When several individuals of the same species are kept together or when several animals are kept together, competition for prime space will be reduced if you

Methods for Creating More Three-dimensional Desert Vivaria

Method 1

Side View

Front View

A single layer of rocks on the same visual plane with plants at the base will give a vivarium a rather flat look.

Method 2

Side View

Front View

Two layers of rock or landscape material with built-up substrate between the rocks or material will give a more interesting three-dimensional design.

Method 3

Side View

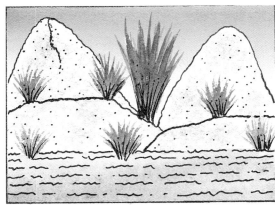

Front View

In a wide vivarium, where three layers of rocks are anchored in the substrate, an even more interesting three-dimensional design can be created.

Illustration by Kevin Anderson.

provide more than one basking area. Dominant, bullying animals may keep subdominant animals away from a basking area; this eventually leads to disease among subdominant animals because they cannot achieve optimal body temperatures, which in turn slows digestion and depresses the efficiency of their immune systems. Of course, you should always design basking areas in relation to overhead light and heat sources such as spotlights.

3. Shelters. The great majority of desert reptiles require some type of shelter, during the blazing heat of the day and as protection at night. Always include shelters in any desert vivaria. Depending on the species you are keeping, you can use human made shelters, including commercial herp shelters, curved roof tiles, and formed concrete shelters; shelters also can be made of overlapping rocks, wood sections, and branch hollows. At least two shelters should be included in any vivarium at varying distances from a heat source. Never place a shelter directly beneath a heat source, as this would defeat its purpose.

Stratifying the Space Within a Vivarium

By using plants, rocks, sections of dead wood, cactus skeleton, and other landscape structures, you can stratify the space within a vivarium. One of the effects of doing so is that you effectively increase the surface area within the vivarium—space on which animals will be able to live and move—by a factor of as much as two or three. Stratifying the space within a vivarium will also cause microclimatic changes in the vivarium landscape.

About Rocks

How often have you gone out into nature and seen rocks that were so beautiful that you have thought about taking them home? Have you ever seen a section of mountain-side, or a wonderful arrangement of rock in a field or on the side of a road, and wished that you could transport that aesthetic effect into your home? As a vivarist you have the opportunity to incorporate some of these rocks in the design of a vivarium and attempt to recreate that section of hill or rock outcropping. Indeed, for dedicated vivarists, the

selection of rocks can be a time-consuming and even a somewhat stressful process. When designing a background for example, with experience you eventually acquire a sense of what types of rocks will work. Finding such rocks can be difficult and can involve sorting through hundreds of rocks at a suppliers. While sorting through rocks, you need to have a mental image of how any rock would look in your vivarium and whether it would suit that space. Once acquired, the right rock can become part of a natural work of art, as are all the other elements in a well-designed vivarium. Rocks are usually among the most important components of a desert vivarium. With carefully selected rocks, relatively few plants are needed to make a desert vivarium look attractive.

Warning: You can easily get injured when looking through bins of rocks at various establishments, so be attentive and take your time. Make sure that when you pull out one rock, it doesn't cause another rock to tumble, possibly crushing your hand or foot!

Several kinds of rocks are available in rock and gravel yards and tropical fish stores. If you live in an area where rocks are readily available, you may be able to collect your own rocks, as long as this is done legally. As a general rule, it is best to avoid mixing different kinds of rocks when designing a vivarium. In nature, desert habitats tend to be associated with particular rock strata.

Some guidelines for the selection of rocks

In vivaria, rocks are used in five ways:

1. As background or background components.
2. As barriers that allow for stratification of the substrata and topography of the vivarium.
3. As basking areas that also add dimensionality to a vivarium.
4. To create shelters.
5. For decorative purposes, to balance the design of a vivarium.

Before you set out to select rocks, you need to ask yourself, "What purpose will the rock I am looking for serve?" Haphazardly selecting rocks on the basis of their visual appeal will not work. You will likely wind up with many rocks that you cannot use when it comes time to design your vivarium.

Selection of rocks

As a general rule, your vivarium will look more natural if you use only one kind of rock in your design. Some vivarists offset the uniformity of the vivarium by adding one very carefully selected rock with a unique aesthetic appeal. Avoid highly abrasive rocks such as some of the volcanic rock sold as lava rock. As these can scrape the skin of reptiles, they can be harmful. For rock-dwelling geckos, use rocks with smooth texture and fine-grained surfaces such as some of the granites, not abrasive rocks such as lava rock or pumice. If in doubt, run your hand or fingers across a rock; this precaution will tell you what kind of surface your animals will have to deal with.

Background rocks

Unless you have a vivarium that is very wide, rocks that are rather thin or flattened are the best choices for backgrounds; otherwise, the rocks will take up too much of the available vivarium space. Because they will be used as backgrounds, those rocks should also be relatively large because your goal will be to cover up a significant portion of the back surface. It is also important that you select rocks with interesting textures. Rocks for backgrounds are

among the most difficult to find, yet the right background rocks can considerably increase the aesthetic appeal of a vivarium.

Rocks for stratifying the vivarium

Rocks for stratification are smaller than background rocks. The best ones are those that have a broad, somewhat flat base and are thinner towards the top. The broad base will give the rocks the stability that will allow you to pack substrate material behind these and the background rocks. Try to select rocks that will tie in visually with the background. Avoid using rocks that are very different from the background rocks.

Basking rocks

Most desert vivaria should have one, and sometimes two, basking rocks. Above the basking rock should be a spotlight. Vivarists will select either rocks that rise significantly above the substrate level or flat rocks that only rise slightly above the substrate. In both cases, the top of any basking rock should provide a broad horizontal-to-semihorizontal surface for lizards to stretch out and bask upon. Remember: the rock should be of such a size that lizards have enough room to move around it when it is placed in the vivarium. Rocks that extend from the front of the vivarium glass all the way to the background rocks seldom work well aesthetically.

Rocks as shelters

When creating shelters using rocks, the standard method is to place a broad flattened rock over a smaller rock, or to place a rock with a flattened bottom over two flattened rocks.

Keeping the rocks in place

To prevent animals or plants from being crushed by rocks accidentally falling or becoming displaced, it is a good idea to use adhesives to keep the rocks firmly where you want them. Background rocks and others can be adhered to the sides of vivaria and to each other with small amounts of

Step by Step Vivarium Design

Step 1. *This 24 inch custom cube vivarium with sliding screen top was designed for keeping collared lizards and small cordylids. It proved attractive and effective. The collared lizards were raised from captive-bred babies and the cordylids were raised from newborns. After the lizards reached adult size, a pair of Moorish geckos was successfully added to the enclosure. In this photo a pitted limestone rock, intended to be the centerpiece of the vivarium, was stabilized by other rocks. Then a layer of coarse pebbles for drainage was added, which further stabilized this structure.*

Step 2. *After spreading the pebble substrate, a growing mix was then added over the drainage layer and between depressions in the rock. A preliminary selection of plants was added: Sansevieria "Gray lady" in the back left, a Mexican caudexed fig (Ficus petiolaris), a couple of Haworthias as well as a small sago palm that turned out to do poorly. Some additional plants were added, including the soft-spined Euphorbia milli var roseana.*

Step 3. *Cork sections for shelters were put in place. The lighting consisted of a single spotlight, so that part of the beam hit the upper portions of the rock and another part reached ground level. In addition, two double-bulb 24-inch fluorescent fixtures with full-spectrum lighting were used to provide adequate light for plants and some beneficial UV light for the lizards.*

Step 4. *A pair of captive-bred collared lizards were captive raised in this vivarium. They have successfully bred.*

clear silicone sealer; however, this type of adhesive will not adhere well to soft limestone or sandstone rocks. Another adhesive that will adhere some types of rock together, but will not work for anchoring rocks to glass, is hot glue applied with a hot-glue gun. You will have to experiment to determine the effectiveness of these adhesives when you design your vivarium. Obviously, you must take care to apply these adhesives in such a way that they are invisible to the vivarium observer.

Decorative balance

Once you have finished placing rocks in a vivarium, the composition will sometimes seem off-balance, as if something else is needed—a rock to be removed, a rock to be added, and so on. Small rocks will often establish a balance in the composition. Another alternative is to select dried sections of wood or some of the attractive sand-blasted woods available in some areas.

About Wood

Most vivarists use rocks as the primary landscape design components of a desert vivarium. A few, however, use dried wood, either as a primary component or as a secondary component.

When wood is used as a primary component, it is commonly because a vivarist has found a section of wood so interesting in texture or natural design that it becomes the centerpiece or focus of the design of the vivarium. With woods, substrate is packed behind the curve of a branch or inside a depression in the wood.

In some vivaria, rocks are used as the primary landscape components while a select piece of wood is used as a basking area; in other cases, a piece of wood may be added to visually balance the design of a vivarium.

Before introducing wood into a desert vivarium

Wood and bark, including cork bark, commonly harbor pests that should not be introduced into a vivarium; these pests may include ants and termites. Placing wood in a large garbage can, adding an entire dichlorvos-impregnated (No-pest) strip, and leaving it overnight will usually kill most insect pests. You must cover the garbage can during the process. Allow the wood to air out for at least 12 hours prior to use.

Types of wood

Reptile stores wanting to emphasize vivarium design will make efforts to stock an interesting selection of wood. Natural driftwoods—both freshwater and saltwater types—sandblasted grape wood, iron wood, and manzanita, as well as cholla and other dried collected wood are available in specialized stores in California and other states with ready access to such materials.

You can also use sections of dry branches or stumps that you have collected. Allow them to dry out thoroughly and treat them for pests, using a dichlorvos-impregnated strip in a large plastic trash can as previously described.

Barks

The rough texture and tan color of cork bark make it well suited to vivarium design. You can partially bury rounded cork bark in the substratum and allow it to serve as a substrate barrier. Cork bark also serves successfully as background and is excellent for the creation of shelters because of its light weight. Other types of dried barks collected from fallen trees can also prove useful in desert vivarium design.

Humidified Shelters

Another important function of shelters is that they provide high relative humidity environments. A primary vehicle for water loss is breathing. Water vapor is exhaled, moving from an area of high relative humidity (inside of the lungs and mouth) to an area of low relative humidity (the outside air). In a shelter, a significant portion of moisture from the soil and/or from exhaled air accumulates, resulting in a high relative humidity environment that will help reduce dehydration rates. The surface areas of shelters in the wild allow for condensation of water which will accumulate at the base. If you have ever lifted rocks or pieces of wood looking for reptiles, you must have noticed that the soil is typically more damp under these natural shelters than out in the open. Studies in the wild on certain geckos have demonstrated that relative humidity is much higher in burrows than above ground. Many desert species will not fare well without shelters and some will require humidified shelters to fare well. Weekly light misting at the base or inside shelters will help raise the relative humidity. Another alternative is to place inside the shelter a small and shallow container with pebbles to which a small amount of water (level must be below the pebble surface) is added. The container should not take up more than a third of the surface area inside the shelter. The evaporation of water from the container will help maintain a higher relative humidity. For several species of lizards, including frog-eyed geckos, humidified shelters can improve their health and facilitate shedding.

Plants for Desert Vivaria

MANY PEOPLE HAVE the mistaken impression that designing a vivarium for amphibians and reptiles is similar to designing a terrarium, except that you add animals to the enclosure. This impression is wrong for the simple reason that a vivarium is designed with the intent of catering to the needs of the animals, and plant selection should be limited to the types of plants that can survive in an enclosure with active animals.

Artificial Plants

A current trend among many dry goods manufacturers is to sell landscape structures with artificial plants, usually silk plants and plastic cacti and succulents. In the authors' opinion,these plants look just like what they are—plastic or silk artificial plants. A vivarium containing these pseudoplants looks artificial, and keeping amphibians and reptiles with such plants can only be termed a form of herpetocultural kitsch (art in poor taste). Because artificial plants are incongruous with the art of vivarium design, the author does *not* recommend them.

Sources of Plants for Desert Vivaria

Sources of desert vivarium plants can be grouped into four categories as follows.

1. Department stores/supermarkets with plant and garden departments. Some of the discount department store chains, such as Target or K-Mart, and hardware/gardening stores, such as Home Depot, have sizable garden departments with good selections of mass-produced succulents and other kinds of plants suitable for desert vivaria. The author has found sansevierias, ponytail palms, gasterias, caudexed figs, and even rarities on occasion in these stores.

2. Specialized nurseries and plant stores. Look in the Yellow Pages and track down nurseries that specialize in cacti and succulents. They commonly have rarer, larger, and more unusual plants than department stores.

3. Mail order. By going to newsstands to find magazines on horticulture such as *Houseplant* and *Horticulture*, you will be able to obtain sources for mail order catalogs and lists. In the author's experience, these are the best sources for unusual sansevierias and desert rarities such as elephant trees *(Bursera)* or caudiciform succulents. Obtaining plants through mail order makes desert vivarium design available to virtually anyone living in the United States. Joining local or national cactus and succulent societies will provide you with access to an even greater selection of plants. Be aware that succulents sold by mail order are usually in sold bare-root form. You should plant these in a well-drained growing medium and water them lightly until they reestablish roots.

4. Vivarium stores. It is the authors' hope that the naturalistic vivarium will catch on and sweep the pet industry by storm. Slowly, you should be seeing increasing numbers of pet stores selling desert vivarium plants.

Before Introducing Live Plants into a Vivarium

When introducing any live plant into a vivarium, whether it is in a pot or not, you must examine the plant carefully for plant pests and for ants. Lift each potted plant out of its pot and inspect the soil and root ball for ants, mealy bugs (white fuzz and small oval whitish bugs), and aphids (tiny greenish bugs that often cluster around the soft parts of a plant). You must remove any ant colonies before introducing plants into a vivarium. One way of safely killing plant pests before introducing plants into a vivarium is to place the plant in a covered garbage can with a dichlorvos-

Sansevieria "Gray Lady"

Sansevieria pinguicula

Sansevieria singularis

Sansevieria sp. GC 81069 Baseball bat

Birdsnest sansevieria: Sansevieria t. "Hahnii"

Sansevieria sp. Mason Congo GC 78133

Sansevieria patens

Sansevieria kirkii

impregnated strip overnight. After treatment, let the plant air out for a day before placing it in the enclosure.

General Rules of Plant Placement in Desert Vivaria

1. Do not overdo the plants. Desert and semiarid areas are not characterized by high plant density. You need to leave space for the landscape structures and for the animals to move about. As a general rule, depending on the animal species and their requirements, plants should occupy from 10 to 30 percent of the surface of the vivarium.

2. Plants should be appropriate in scale. Your vivarium plants should have a height at least equal to the height of the animals that you are keeping (when they are at rest),

preferably considerably taller. This is not a set rule; with lizards such as geckos, which are unlikely to cause much damage, you can use shorter plants.

3. The tallest plants should be placed in the back. In some cases you can place tall plants along the side near the front to increase the dimensionality of a design. You can also place tall plants in the middle area of a vivarium, to increase dimensionality or to split the vivarium into two topographic sections. It is generally recommended that tall plants *not* be placed in the front of a vivarium; they tend to block the view of everything behind them. Again, this is not a set rule. Placing one or two tall plants near the front of a vivarium can increase the topographical dimensionality of design.

4. Smaller plants go in front. You should always place small plants in front of taller ones, except when they can be placed high in the landscape near the lights at a level above that of taller plants.

5. Place your plants as they grow in nature. Remember that many plants in deserts are found at the base of rocks or between rocks. Rocks that cover part of the substrate will reduce evaporation rates in desert areas; plants at the base of rocks will also obtain water—from moisture that condenses on rocks and that eventually forms water droplets, which drip to the base. In vivaria, plants at the base of rocks or between rocks will give a natural, aesthetic, three-dimensional appearance to the vivarium.

6. Avoid using too many different plants. Plants in the wild typically occur in groupings. A habitat suitable for a species of plant will usually contain more than one plant of

Sansevieria "golden Hahnii"

Sansevieria subspicata

Sansevieria subspicata, fan form

Sansevieria trifasciata

Sansevieria t. "Moonshine"

Sansevieria "Bantel's Sensation"

that species. Good designs usually have several specimens of smaller species and one or possibly more specimens of taller plants, depending on the vivarium size.

An Overview of Plant Species Suitable for Desert Vivaria

The following are plant species that the author has tried and that have been successful in desert vivaria.

· **Snakeplants** *(Sansevieria)*

Snakeplants are so variable and have such interesting sculptural forms, subtle patterns, and colors that vivarists quickly become part of the growing number of sansevieria aficionados. Before long, you may find yourself having snakeplants not only in vivaria but in most rooms of your house. The decorative effect of some of these plants—with their simplicity of lines and thick-leaved characteristics— are hard to beat. They are the favorite plants of vivarists who own desert vivaria. They propagate vegetatively by offsets, which means that single plants planted in a pot will eventually fill that pot. They do best in bright indirect light, so don't place them near spotlights or they will burn. They require a well-drained soil or they will rot at their bases.

The following are some of the many species available through mail order. In most areas of the United States, only the common snake plant, sansevieria "Moonshine," and birdsnest sansevieria are readily available in plant departments of various stores. Your best chance of obtaining the more sculptural species is to get them through mail order. Unfortunately, with the slow-growing thick-leaved species, demand is bound to exceed supply.

· **Tall flat-leafed snakeplants**

Common snakeplant (*Sansevieria trifasciata* and cultivars)
Sansevieria "Bantel's Sensation"
Sansevieria "Gray Lady"
Sansevieria "Moonshine"
Sansevieria metallica
Sansevieria zeylanica

· **Short flat-leafed snakeplants**

Birdsnest sansevieria (*Sansevieria t.* Hahnii) many cultivars
· **Semicylindrical- to cylindrical-leafed snakeplants**
Sansevieria aethiopica
Sansevieria sp. " Baseball bat" (outstanding!)
Sansevieria caniculata
Sansevieria cylindrica (dwarf forms are preferable)
Sansevieria singularis (highly recommended)
Many others

Note: Several cylindrical sansevierias have sharp points at the ends of their leaves. You should clip these off, using a nail clipper.

· **Caudiciforms**

Caudiciform plants form an arbitrary grouping of primarily arid- to semiarid-habitat plants characterized by a *caudex*, a swollen stem that serves as a water-storage organ. Their natural bonsai forms make them some of the most attractive plants that you can grow in a vivarium. The number of caudiciform enthusiasts is many times greater than that of sansevieria collectors. Some of these plants have an other-worldly look. The following is an overview of some species that will work in desert vivaria.

· **Ponytail palms**
(Beaucarnea recurvata)
The interesting, hardy members of the lily family known as ponytail palms are readily available and thrive in vivaria. If you keep them in small pots and do not water them too

A succulent arrid, Zamioculcas zamiifolia.

frequently, their growth will be slow and you will be able to enjoy them in your vivarium for years.

· **Caudexed figs**

Two species from Mexico, *Ficus petiolaris* and *Ficus palmeri*, are readily available through mail order and in the nursery sections of department stores in some parts of the country. These small trees are easily grown in desert vivaria and with regular pruning can become outstanding bonsai. Because figs leak a latex when damaged, do *not* use them in a vivarium with large scratching, crushing species of reptiles.

oft-spined crown of thorns, Euphorbia illi var roseana.

· **Elephant trees** (*Bursera*)

Members of the genus *Bursera* sold by succulent growers are thick-stemmed aromatic shrubs that grow into natural bonsai forms. The easiest species to grow in vivaria is *Bursera hindsiana*. Other species, such as *Bursera fagaroides* and *B. microphyllla* , are touchier; *B. microphyllla* is especially difficult.

· **Caudexed cucurbits**

Several caudexed members of the squash family can be grown in vivaria with insect-eating lizards. One species that has worked for the senior author is *Gerardanthus macrorhizus*. The advantage of these caudiciforms is that they can make vinelike growth in the vivarium. The disadvantages are that they can be invasive and therefore require regular pruning; also, several species are poisonous.

· **Bromeliads**

Several bromeliad species could fare well in desert vivaria; the problem is that species adapted to desert conditions—*Dyckia* and *Puya*, for example, tend to be spiny and therefore potentially harmful to desert reptiles. Many members of the genus *Cryptanthus*, popularly called earth stars, will usually thrive in desert vivaria. Because many of the forms sold in the plant trade are quite colorful, they can add interest to any desert vivarium. Some of the tillandsias adapted to more arid conditions will work well also. These should be attached to dry wood sections placed close to fluorescent bulbs. One test for more arid-adapted bromeliads is to run your finger along the leaf edge. If it feels like you could get pricked by a particular bromeliad, then so could reptiles kept in vivaria containing these plants.

· **Euphorbias**

Some of the most diverse and interesting of plants are the members of the genus *Euphorbia*. Most people are familiar with the poinsettia, the cactuslike *Euphorbia*, and the crown of thorns. Other species resemble what one would imagine to be plants from other planets: some look like natural bonsai trees (for example, *Euphorbia misera* from Baja California and some forms of *Euphorbia balsamifera*); others

Mexican caudexed fig, Ficus petiolaris.

South African xerophytic orchid, Eulophia petersii.

A vining caudexed asclepiad, Raphionacme flanangani.

San Pedro cactus (Trichocereus pachanoi).

resemble odd potato like tubers with peculiar short growths; still others look like odd, thickened crinkly-leafed herbs, and so on. There are many plant collectors who find *Euphorbias* so interesting that they specialize only in plants of that genus.

Fortunately, there are several species of *Euphorbia* that will fare well in vivaria. There are also certain rules with *Euphorbias*. Because all *Euphorbias* release a white latex that can be harmful if it comes in contact with eyes and, in some species, with skin, they can be used only with smaller reptiles, which are unlikely to scratch or damage the plants. You could use some of the larger species with larger animals, but to do so you will need large room-size enclosures or outdoor enclosures. Also, many of the *Euphorbias* have high light requirements. Species that will tolerate lower light levels will generally fare better in vivaria.

Euphorbias—particularly some of the Madagascar species such as *E. decaryi* , *E. francoisii,* and *E. cylindripholia*—are interesting low-growing plants that you can grow in vivaria with very small reptiles; *E. milloti* will also work well under these conditions.

· Cow tongues or ox tongues *(Gasteria)*
Under a four-lightbulb regimen, these thick-leaved, slow-growing members of the lily family will thrive in vivaria. Some species have sharp, pointed tips that you should clip if you are to use them in vivaria.

· Haworthias
Many of these small liliaceous African succulents fare reasonably well under desert vivarium light regimens, particularly in low vivaria. In taller vivaria you should provide at least four fluorescent lights. The most readily available species is the aristocrat plant *(Haworthia fasciata),* but others are occasionally sold in plant stores, and many species are available from mail order succulent nurseries. Some, such as the slow-growing *H. margaritifera* (with raised white spots) and *H. browniana,* are impressive. Others, such as the cylindrical-leafed *H. maughanii* and the thick, flat-leafed *H. truncata,* are geometrical marvels.

Some, such as *H. cymbiformis,* have a bright, semitranslucent yellow-green coloration. You can find many interesting short plants for the desert vivarium in this genus. Soft-leafed species, such as *H. bolusii* and *H cymbiformis,* will be easily damaged by reptiles and can only be used with small species or geckos. As a rule, Haworthias fare best in vivaria when they are maintained in pots. The authors have had mixed results with these plants and recommend that you first experiment with some of the less expensive species.

· Aloes
Most aloes have high light requirements but some (mostly dwarf species) will fare well in vivaria. Some species that are recommended are *Aloe variegata, Aloe aristata, Aloe ciliaris, Aloe jucunda,* and *Aloe rauhii.* Larger species tend to outgrow vivaria.

· Grapes
There are several succulent species of grapes: some are thick-stemmed vines *(Cissus quadrangularis);* others form a caudex *(Cyphostemma species).*

· Ceropegias
These mostly succulent and tuberous vining members of the milkweed family can be useful if you are looking for plants with vinelike growth. The best known is rosary vine *(Ceropegia woodii).* Several species are available through mail order. One of the best is *Ceropegia sandersoni,* with large parachute-shaped flowers. *Ceropegia dichotoma* has thick vertical stems.

· Cacti
Based on the author's experiments, the use of most cacti in desert vivaria is discouraged. They tend to be dangerously spiny, and/or etiolate (explanation follows listing of plants), and seldom fare well under vivarium conditions. The most successful species for these vivaria is *Consolea falcata,* a flat-leafed, dark green, and nearly spineless species. Other spineless flat-padded cacti also tend to succeed. One species of nearly spineless columnar cactus that will grow well in a well-lit vivarium is San Pedro cactus *(Trichocereus pachanoi).*

A close-up of a desert vivarium setup. With smaller reptiles that do not eat plants, latex-generating species such as euphorbias and potentially poisonous species can be utilized in vivaria. Be sure to use common sense in your selection.

A close-up of an enclosure showing stacked rocks as shelters and basking sites.

The clown agama (Laudakia stellio brachydactyla) is a beautiful species that tends to fare better than most of the other imported "agamas." They are ideal candidates for naturalistic vivaria.

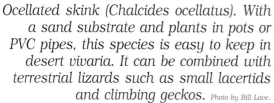

Another desert set-up using the buried-pot method, designed for keeping collared lizards. The enclosure is a 48-inch breeder cage by Neodesha Plastics®. Photo by Val Brinkerhoff.

Ocellated skink (Chalcides ocellatus). With a sand substrate and plants in pots or PVC pipes, this species is easy to keep in desert vivaria. It can be combined with terrestrial lizards such as small lacertids and climbing geckos. Photo by Bill Love.

Armadillo lizard (Cordylus cataphractus). Most members of the cordylid family will thrive in desert vivaria with stacked securely fastened horizontal rocks. Photo by Bill Love.

A five-foot front-opening vivarium with agamas, collared lizards, frog-eyed geckos, and Moorish geckos.

A desert vivarium designed by Small Worlds Vivarium in 1978 in an architect's office. No plants were used. The background was custom made and consisted of rocks and cork bark embedded in epoxy resin. Photo by Vern French.

This helmeted gecko Geckonia chazaliae is a species that will fare well in desert vivaria. Photo by Bill Love.

*A desert vivarium with plants potted in the substrate
and pea gravel as a top layer containing geraniums
and pony-tail palm.*

A close-up of an enclosure showing the use of a
buried concrete shelter and cork bark to create
hiding places.

plantless vivarium at White Mountain unior High School housing Egyptian romastyx (Uromastyx aegyptius). Only izeable tall plants such as large pony-tail alms or yuccas would be likely to survive ne intense digging activity and nibbling of nese vegetarian lizards. Photo by Val Brinkerhoff.

Round-tailed horned lizard (Phrynosoma modestum). This species is still collected in some numbers for the pet trade. If they are exposed to sunlight or a source of UVB, they will do reasonably well on a diet of cultured fruit flies (Drosophila hydei), mealworms, and small crickets, with the fruit flies forming the bulk of the diet. These lizards are only recommended for experienced keepers. Photo by Bill Love.

An overhead view of an open-top custom-made desert vivarium for bearded dragons. This enclosure was designed by Dan McCarron at White Mountain Junior High School. Dan is the organizer of the annual AFH-sponsored workshop for teachers, "Herpetoculture in the classroom."

A side view of the above vivarium. Dragon trees (Dracaena marginata) were successfully used in these large enclosures.

Photos by Val Brinkerhoff.

A four-foot front-opening vivarium. Sansevierias, the nearly spineless, padded cactus Consolea falcata and an elephant tree (center, Bursera hindsiana) were included in the design.

esigned for frog-eyed eckos (Teratoscincus scincus), the sansevierias in this ivarium were planted in a growing medium ith a top layer of fine pea gravel.

This vivarium with plants in the growing layer was designed by the author for "The Forgotten Forest" in 1984. It utilized a special hood that combined incandescent spotlights and four full-spectrum fluorescent bulbs. This was an experiment in combining plant diversity with animals. The plants included potentially toxic species, such as sea onion (Boweia volubilis) and several Euphorbia. Other plants include (to the back right) pony-tail palm (Beaucarnea recurvata), a dwarf century plant (Agave in the center), aloes, and haworthias. Most fared well long-term under the high-light regimen. Two species of lizards were kept in this vivarium: leopard geckos which emerged at night and a medium-size species of Lacerta.

A desert vivarium combining limestone rock and petrified wood.

Veiled chameleon (Chamaeleo calyptratus). Some species of chameleons from arid areas could be kept in tall desert-type vivaria. Food should be offered in ceramic or plastic feeding dishes. A sandy soil is the best surface substrate. *Photo by Bill Love.*

This frog-eyed gecko was successfully bred in a desert vivarium.

...any lacertids from ...y areas are good ...oices for desert ...aria. This species, ...e jeweled lacerta ...certa lepida), is ...ptive-bred in small ...mbers in the United ...tes. *Photo by Bill Love.*

Inland bearded dragons (Pogona vitticeps) are good candidates for desert vivaria, but they will eat and damage plants within easy reach. *Photo by Corey Blanc.*

A 24-inch cube vivarium designed for collared lizards and small cordylids.

A 30-inch long front-opening vivarium with plants placed directly in the growing substrate. This enclosure was designed for medium-size desert species such as collared lizards and cordylids. The background plants are sansevieria. In the foreground are small aloes. Achieving an aesthetic balance between plants and landscape structures is important. Remember to combine rock work, shelters, and open space. Two-to-five plants are often all that are needed to give a naturalistic feel to a desert vivarium.

Another cube-type vivarium with sansevieria and haworthia. Only three plants were used to give this vivarium a naturalistic effect. Overplanting can be unattractive and can fail to provide the open spaces needed by many desert species.

· Orchids

There are some near-succulent orchids that will fare well in desert vivaria. One outstanding, although expensive, species is *Eulopia petersii*, which has pseudo bulbs and rigid leaves.

· Ornamental flowering plants

Ornamental flowering plants can add a very appealing aesthetic element to vivaria. You can use two approaches. One is to add flowering plants to a vivarium on a temporary basis, reserving specific areas for these temporary additions. The other is to select plants that have brightly colored flowers and that can flower readily in a vivarium.

For desert vivaria, some of the best candidates are some of the dwarf crown-of-thorns species (such as *Euphorbia milli v. roseana*), which have few spines or spines soft enough that they are unlikely to injure any of the animals. Euphorbias with wide leaves such as *E. milloti* will work well too.

Some of the commercial red- or orange-flowered kalanchoes also may flourish in vivarium conditions. You should place these plants in such a manner that their growing ends can be as close as possible to lights, so that they will flower.

· Geraniums (*Pelargonium* species)

Geraniums usually grow well and flower in desert vivaria, many species and varieties are available. Small-leafed, heat-tolerant types will be the best choices. Many interesting, very succulent, and thick-stemmed species of geranium are highly sought by plant collectors. Unfortunately, many of these species are dormant in summer, usually dropping all their foliage at that time and requiring little water. *Pelargonium carnosum* is one of the hardier thick-stemmed succulent species for use in vivaria. Nonetheless, there is such a large selection of these plants that there are several species that will thrive and enhance the appearance of your desert vivarium.

· Trees and miscellaneous species

There are many other plant species suited to desert vivaria, but they would require an entire booklet for proper coverage. (We are working on it.) Several species of trees

Purchased plants may be in pots too deep to fit in the substrate layer of your vivarium. An alternative is to transfer the plants to shallow food storage containers.

These plants are ready to transfer to a vivarium.

Drill holes in the bottom of the storage containers and transfer the plants, adding well drained growing medium, if necessary. A wider food container will allow for better root spread, more substrate, and better plant growth.

will work, including acacia and other leguminous trees, olive trees (*Olea*), thin- or thick-leafed dragon trees, various figs (*Ficus*), as well as shrubs. There are many more succulent and caudiciform plants. Obviously, species adaptable to indirect, rather than direct, sunlight will fare best. Species that do not grow very large or that you can keep small by pruning are also good choices. Avoid species that release a latex when injured, and avoid using poisonous species with omnivorous or vegetarian reptiles. The selection possibilities are virtually limitless, and the potential of plants for creating strikingly beautiful vivaria may surprise you.

Etiolation

Plants exposed to insufficient light, particularly cacti and succulents, will demonstrate spindly, usually pale growth, which can deform their appearance. In horticulture, this process is known as etiolation. Because it ruins the appearance and generally weakens the plants, it is important to select plants that show normal growth under the lighting you have selected for your vivarium. If lights are

low, play it safe and go with some of the sansevierias or haworthias. With plants requiring more light, landscape your vivarium so that they are closer to the fluorescent bulbs. Many typical cacti etiolate (become pale and "leggy") in a vivarium, which is why they are among the more difficult plants to keep under desert vivarium conditions.

Hand sprayers are useful for watering individual plants, for misting and humidifying the inside of shelters.

Watering Plants in a Desert Vivarium

Water your plants in a desert vivarium at the base only, using a handpump-type sprayer or a baster. You must *never* water the

entire substrate surface of a desert vivarium. If plants are in pots, simply add water to the pot. Add enough water to permeate to the ends of the roots. Remember: with cacti and succulents, it is a good idea to allow some time for them to dry out before you water them again. These are not tropical forest species. For most desert vivarium species, watering every seven to ten days will usually be adequate, although it is best to adjust your watering according to the condition of the plants

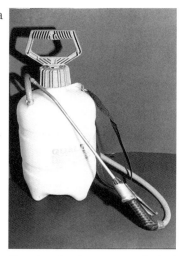

Pump type hand sprayers are the best choice for hand watering individual plants, particularly if one has several vivaria.

and the soil medium. Very dry or very wet weather can affect the amount of moisture in the soil of a vivarium. There are electronic soil-moisture testers that can help. But usually, simply observing the plants will inform you if your regimen is correct. Underwatered plants will show some shriveling. Overwatered plants may split; they also may rot or appear to be dying because their roots have rotted as a result of lengthy exposure to a soggy medium. During winter months, at cooler temperatures and shorter day lengths, succulents and cacti should be watered less frequently because most of them will undergo a period of dormancy during this time. (There are cool weather winter growers, however.)

Succulent Plant Rot

When you overwater succulent plants or keep them in a soil with poor drainage, there is an increased chance of rot, typically caused by fungi. It is a good idea, therefore, to be conservative when you water these moisture-retaining plants.

Winter Dormancy

Most succulent plants become dormant in cool weather and need to be kept drier during the winter months or they will rot. With the few species that are winter growers, you should increase watering when these plants demonstrate the first signs of growth.

Plant Maintenance

One of the features to expect of plants in a well-designed desert vivarium is that they will grow and/or spread. This process is part of what the naturalistic vivarium concept is about. Initially, plants will grow or offset, thereby improving the original design of the vivarium by giving it a more established look, Eventually, however, these plants will probably grow too large to maintain the balance that should be your goal. Tall plants will likely block out light and push up against the screen top. Other plants may spread so much that the animals have little room in which to move. To prevent overgrowth, you must prune and remove plant divisions or rhizomes as it becomes necessary. If the plants are potted in pieces of PVC pipe or pots, the containers will prevent the spread or division. One of the positive results of pruning certain shrubby or tree-like plants is that inadvertently you will be creating bonsai in your vivarium.

Step by Step Vivarium Design

Pitted limestone rock and a drainage layer are added to a 36 inch tank.

A commercial cactus growing medium is mixed with pumice to increase drainage.

The growing medium is added to the vivarium and spread so that it is thicker where plants will be placed, such as at the base of rocks or in corners. The plants are then added: Haworthia, odd species of geranium, Euphorbia milli var roseana (back left) and Sansevieria singularis.

The complete vivarium, designed for keeping frog-eyed geckos (Teratoscincus kyserlingii) and Jones armadillo lizards (Cordylus jonesi). The frog-eyed geckos have fared well in this particular setup.

Jone's armadillo lizards (Cordylus jonesi) in the same vivarium as the frog-eyed geckos. The two species were compatible.

Practice Makes Better

Vivarium design is a form of art that requires experience with the component media. A vivarium is an enclosed manmade landscape that simulates some of the essential elements of an animal's habitat in a way that meets the needs of the animals and the human observer as well. The palette of the vivarist consists not of paints, but of the elements assembled to form the final composition. These elements should include bags or boxes of substrata; boxes of dried woods, stumps, roots, and small tree bases; boxes of bark; branches; boxes of rocks; and plant trays with an assortment of plants. Without a good selection of vivarium elements, you will not be able to design an attractive vivarium, so your first step should be to gather all the necessary elements. Doing this will take work and time, but the care you take in selecting the landscape components will be a key factor in the outcome and success of your final design.

As with any art, some individuals will feel more at ease than others in selecting and assembling these elements to design a vivarium. Some people seem generally more talented than others, yet the basic skill of vivarium design will be acquired *only* with practice and experience. Your first attempt at designing a vivarium may not work well or look great, but do not become discouraged. Maintain the confidence to try again. After you have designed several vivaria, you will get better at it and possibly become an artist with a vision. A good vivarium artist eventually acquires a sense of design that almost intuitively combines aesthetics with the creation of vivarium niches for animals.

Vivarium Maturation

Naturalistic vivaria are not static. When conditions are right, as a result of the plants used in its design, a vivarium grows, changes, and matures into a more aesthetically pleasing display. Typically, the plants fill out or produce offsets; they also grow in relation to the landscape and lighting. The end result in a well-designed desert vivarium is that it usually will look even better a year later than it did when it was originally set up. If the vivarium looks worse a year after it was set up, then the selection of plants and landscaping may have been wrong for the animals you are keeping. Because of their size and activity, some reptiles will eventually trash almost any landscape you design, which is why very large naturalistic vivaria are recommended for larger lizards.

Close-up showing some of the sansevierias in this desert vivarium.

Hardware

WARNING: BEFORE elaborating on the hardware used with desert vivaria, you need to know about the use of lights and heating elements required. If used or placed improperly, these light- and heat-generating devices can cause electrocution and fires. Use good judgment; *always* think about fire prevention. If you place a 150-watt spotlight in a reflector-type fixture near curtains, it could cause a fire, particularly if the family cat accidentally topples it. Any combustible substance in close contact with a hot reflector could catch on fire. Short circuits or misuse of heating systems can also cause fires and electrocution. Keep all electrical systems away from water. Worst-case scenario: the bottom of your all-glass enclosure cracks, the subtank heater is damaged, and the water in the drainage layer drains, forming a puddle over the heater.

Common-sense precautions are to plug all vivarium units into a surge-suppressor outlet and to install one smoke alarm in every room containing vivaria. Several accidents occur each year that are associated with the misuse of vivarium- or reptile-related equipment. A little common sense can go a long way toward preventing such accidents.

> Check the placement and installation of all heating and lighting components. Install a smoke alarm in any room containing vivaria.

Kenya sand boa
(Eryx colubrinus loveridgei).

These small boas will do extremely well in naturalistic vivaria with sand substrate.
Photo by Bill Love.

Lighting

Lighting is a critical factor in the design of a desert vivarium. In order for desert vivaria to thrive, relatively large amounts of lights are required. Any desert vivarium will require two to three types of light:

1. Lighting for general illumination, strong enough to allow for the growth of plants. As a rule, at least four full-spectrum fluorescent bulbs running the length of the vivarium are necessary for growing live plants in a desert vivarium. Plants requiring high light intensities fare best when placed close to the bulbs. You can use individual small spotlights to provide extra light to such plants.

2. Incandescent basking lights [see *Heating*] that will heat specific basking areas in the vivarium. These lights are necessary to allow the animals to thermoregulate.

3. BL-type blacklights. The main feature of these bulbs is their high ultraviolet-A (UV-A) output, which benefits many species, particularly those that have ultraviolet vision. A study on the desert iguana, for example, has shown that

Reflector-type incandescent fixtures capable of safely handling at least 150-watt spotlights are a requirement for most desert vivaria set up in homes. Always be extremely careful as to the placement and secure positioning of these lights or there can be a risk of fire.

If a light is placed close to the ground or close to a basking site, a horizontal heat gradient can be established, whereby the animal can thermoregulate through horizontal activity. Illustration by Kevin Anderson.

the benefits of UV-A may be both behavioral and physical. With some species, UV-A may indirectly assist calcium absorption.

We recommend at least one BL-black light with desert reptiles. This bulb can replace one of the four fluorescent bulbs.

A word about new lighting systems: some metal halide and self-ballasted mercury bulbs generate a desirable spectral range that includes UV-B, the ultraviolet radiation that appears to be necessary for many reptiles to synthesize their own vitamin D_3. They also generate significant levels of UV-A. One problem with them, however, is that in addition to light, they generate a considerable amount of

If a light is placed over branches in a tall vivarium, there will be a milder horizontal heat gradient but a more significant vertical heat gradient. An animal can thermoregulate through vertical positioning. Illustration by Kevin Anderson.

heat. Nevertheless, if you place them at an appropriate height (determined with the aid of a thermometer), these lights may prove very valuable in maintaining reptiles that come from dry areas with high light intensity. Plant growth under these high-intensity lights will be excellent.

Always use a shield with UV-generating bulbs—whether BL-type blacklights, metal halides, or mercury vapor—to help protect humans from UV exposure.

Timers Used to Control the Photoperiod

In a vivarium, the easiest way to control the photoperiod (daily exposure to light, which in vivaria also includes daytime heat) is to set the lights on timers. Electric plug-in timers are readily available in drug stores and hardware stores. For two-pronged light fixtures, such as spotlights, you can use standard outlet timers; for three-pronged fluorescent fixtures, you will need three-pronged appliance timers.

The standard practice is to set timers so that lights are on 14 hours per day for most of the year. During the winter months, usually from December 15 to February 15, herpetoculturists reduce the photoperiod to 10 hours per day while also cooling daytime and nighttime temperatures. Follow instructions in books and manuals for cooling the species you are keeping.

**UV GENERATING FLUORESCENT BULBS
RECOMMENDED BY THE AUTHOR**

    ESU Reptile Daylight

    Flukers- ReptaSun

    Zoo Med- Reptisun UVB310

The extra UVB output can be of significant benefit to desert reptiles.

Heating

THERE SHOULD BE two sources of heat in a desert vivarium; one generated by incandescent bulbs and another generated by subtank heat units. The standard design approach for desert lizards is to place spotlights in reflectors above basking areas to create a heat gradient.

One of the effects of this arrangement is that the heat lessens as the animal moves farther from the center of a bulb. Yet at the same time, enough heat is generated that the overall air temperature in the vivarium is increased. Always place shelters away from direct exposure to spotlights. As a general rule, when overhead light (comparable to the radiant heat from the sun) is used, the temperature inside a shelter will be significantly cooler than that on exposed surface areas.

Another type of heating system recommended for desert vivaria is a subtank heater, or a heat source beneath the substrate. Unfortunately, the effectiveness of subtank heaters will depend on the types of substrates used. Subtank heat will not move effectively through dense substrates, which actually create an insulation layer; however, it will move well through a coarse substrate with air flow between the particles. With the coarse substrate, it will generate heat at night, when temperatures tend to become too low. One feature of substrate heat is that it tends to accumulate inside shelters, causing the shelters to act as heat traps. Any substrate heater should be on a thermostat and adjusted to the desired temperature, using probes inside the shelters. Tropic Zone®, Flex Watt®, Ultratherm®, ZooMed®, and others produce subtank heating units suitable for desert vivaria. Rheostatic or thermostatic controls are recommended for all of these units.

Hot-Rock-type Heaters

Hot-rock-type heaters can be useful as secondary heat sources in vivaria and particularly useful for geckos which are active at night. They generally can be left on around the clock. Select hot rocks with a surface temperature of about 85° F (29.4° C). It is highly recommended that you use a thermometer with a probe with hot-rock-type heaters. Even more recommended are hot-rock-type heaters with temperature-control units.

Some Principles of Heat Distribution in Desert Vivaria

Subtank heating causes heat to rise from the bottom of the tank through the glass, through the substrate, and upward. If the heat encounters dense material, it will have trouble penetrating it to reach areas above; if the material is airy, the heat will be able to move up more readily. With subtank heaters, dense substrates limit the ability of heat to reach the surface, whereas airy substrates allow the heat to reach the surface. Thus, with subtank heaters, the less thick the substrate the greater the heat will be at the surface, all other factors being equal.

Finally, when you install subtank heaters, shelters on the surface will act as heat traps; the temperature inside the shelter will be greater than that of the surrounding environment. For this reason, substrate heating for heating vivaria at night is recommended when the weather is cool. Many vivarists keep substrate heaters off during the day and set them on timers to come on at night, thereby allowing animals in shelters to keep warmer on cool nights. The author recommends a rheostat or thermostat, as well as a thermometer with a probe, for the proper setup and monitoring of these heating systems.

Vivarium Controls

DEPENDING UPON THE species you are keeping, the area you live in, and the climate controls of your house, you will need one or more instruments for controlling and monitoring the microclimate of your vivarium. Because temperature and relative humidity can vary significantly over the course of a year (the air is dry and temperatures are cooler in the winter as a result of central heating, for example), microclimatic control can be critical to the survival of your animals.

Equipment

Depending upon how sophisticated you want your vivaria to be, you can purchase a variety of monitoring equipment. The very minimum monitoring device you should purchase is an electronic digital-readout thermometer with an external probe. These thermometers can be purchased through electronic supply stores such as Radio Shack®. A digital thermometer with a probe allows you to have a readout of the low temperature in a vivarium (the temperature farthest away from the light sources), as well as of the basking area. As alternatives, inexpensive glass-enclosed thermometers and temperature-sensitive strips are now sold in many pet stores.

Hygrometers

For measuring relative humidity, an electronic digital hygrometer can prove quite useful. These can be purchased though scientific supply companies such as Edmund Scientific. Wet-bulb-type hygrometers and relative-humidity-sensitive strips are also available and usually are more economical than digital readout hygrometers.

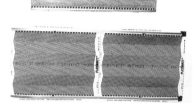

There are now several kinds of subtank heating systems for reptiles sold in the pet trade. Always follow instructions to prevent fires and cracked glass bottoms. Ideally the heating pads or strips should be connected to a rheostat or a thermostat.

Timers are essential vivarium hardware. Incandescent bulbs should be on two-prong timers but shop lights or other three-prong electrical equipment should be on three prong timers.

Several thermostats for regulating reptile heating systems are now on the market. This is a programmable day/night on-off thermostat.

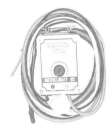

This is an example of a pulse proportional thermostat. Another brand the author recommends is Helix Controls®.

A light meter can be used to determine light intensity in a vivarium. This can be particularly useful when keeping certain kinds of plants.

A digital thermometer with external probe.

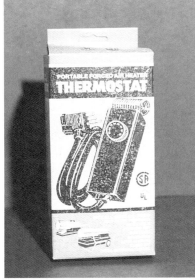

Heaters in reptile rooms should be connected to a thermostatic system to prevent overheating.

A digital thermometer and hygrometer with external temperature probe.

In vivaria with subtank heating, shelters will trap heat and the temperature inside the shelter may exceed outside temperature. The thermometer on the right has a probe inside the hollow concrete shelter to its left.

Cooling

The only effective method of cooling a vivarium is to use lower wattage spotlights and to turn down subtank heaters. If the room containing your vivarium is too warm, open windows or use an air conditioner. There are few alternatives.

Heat Controls

Many herpetoculturists use rheostats (light dimmers or fan regulators) to control subtank heaters, incandescent lighting, and/or ceramic infrared heating bulbs. Always use a rheostat that has the capacity to handle the wattage of the equipment you are regulating. Follow the manufacturer's instructions and words of caution. Some manufacturers, such as Ultratherm®, sell rheostat-type controllers to regulate their subtank heaters/reptile heating pads.

On/off thermostats

These thermostats turn heating systems on and off as needed to maintain the temperature at the probe level. Some of the newer thermostats, such as Reptile Custom Network®, are programmable, so that you can set different temperatures for day and night.

Pulse-proportional thermostats

The best thermostats for vivaria are the pulse-proportional types, which essentially dim incandescent lighting and lower the temperatures of subtank heaters; these thermostats are preferable to the less expensive on/off thermostats. Microclimate Electronix® and Helix Controls® manufacture high-quality pulse-proportional thermostats used by many herpetoculturists.

Vivarium Maintenance

Besides the maintenance schedule required for keeping animals alive and healthy, vivaria should be maintained on a weekly basis. For desert vivaria, this involves the following steps *on a weekly basis.*

1. Scoop out feces visible on the surface of the substrate using a tool such as a cat litter scoop or a small strainer. Custom-made scoops or strainers can be built depending on the requirements of your enclosure.

2. Check plants for signs of disease; prune them as needed, and water them at the base. Remove sick or damaged plants and replace them.

3. Clean glass with a glass cleaner containing either ammonia or vinegar. Wipe glass dry after cleaning.

4. Add water to humidified shelters.

5. Check heating, lighting, and control equipment to make sure all are working properly.

6. Keep notes on your vivarium concerning temperature range, relative humidity, and the status of animals and plants; also on the vivarium as a display.

Excessive Food Insects

If you introduce into a vivarium more live insects than the reptiles will eat at a sitting, the insects typically hide or burrow. In the long run, the insects become hungry and decide to eat the plants in the vivarium, thus ruining their visual appeal. King mealworms and their beetles will eat cork and eventually turn an attractive piece of cork into something resembling Swiss cheese. Don't offer reptiles more insects than they can eat at one feeding; whenever possible, offer the feeder insects in shallow dishes that minimize their escape into the vivarium.

Very small arid habitat tortoises such as the Egyptian tortoise (Testudo Kleinmanni) can be kept in desert vivaria. Photo by Bill Love.

Animals for Desert Vivaria

THE STANDARD RULES of herpetoculture regarding new animals apply when you are setting up a desert vivarium. First, select the healthiest animals available at the time of your purchase (see *The Lizard Keeper's Handbook* by de Vosjoli). Next, you must quarantine your animals and acclimate them to captivity in simple but proper setups.

General Rules Prior to Introduction of Animals into Desert Vivaria

Experienced vivarists quarantine their animals for 60 to 90 days before introducing them into a naturalistic vivarium. They check and treat their animals for external parasites. They also have fecal samples examined by a qualified reptiled veterinarian and treat their animals for any internal parasites. These precautions simply make good sense. To treat sick animals in a naturalistic vivarium is difficult. If an animal has a gastroenteric infection or internal parasites, part of its treatment will involve maintaining that animal on a clean, easy-to-change substrate—usually newspaper. It is very difficult to treat a condition if the animals are initially kept in a naturalistic vivarium. To prevent reinfection, you would have to take apart the entire vivarium and put it back together only after disinfecting rock work and landscape structures, replacing the substrates, and thoroughly washing all live plants. You would have to perform the same procedures if the animals are infected with mites.

The wiser approach is prevention—through quarantining and first establishing the animals in more simply designed vivaria with easily replaced substrates. The risk of disease is reduced if the animals are captive-bred, but it is not eliminated completely. The author has bought groups of captive-bred leopard geckos and bearded dragons that were later discovered to be infected with coccidia. Obvi-ously, how the breeder or pet store keeps animals can also a factor. By carefully selecting your animals, whether imported or captive-bred, you can reduce the probability of disease, but introducing animals into a vivarium without prior quarantine will always be a serious and generally unwise gamble.

The following is a list of some reptiles that will fare well in suitably designed desert vivaria. To determine their requirements, refer to any of the many books now available in the trade, particularly species-specific books and *The Lizard Keeper's Handbook* by Philippe de Vosjoli.

Geckos

Middle Eastern dwarf geckos: *Tropiocolotes (Microgecko)* and *Stenodactylus* species

Leopard geckos (*Eublepharis macularius*)

Fat-tail geckos (*Hemitheconyx caudicinctus*)

Desert banded geckos (*Coleonyx*)

Crocodile geckos (*Tarentola mauritanica*)

White-spotted geckos (*Tarentola annularis*)

Fan-footed geckos (*Ptyodactylus hasselquistii*)

Frog-eyed geckos (*Teratoscincus* sp.)

Chondrodactylus

Palmatogecko

Eyelash geckos and relatives: *Diplodactylus ciliaris* and other species

Agamids

Many *Agama* species

Bearded dragons (*Pogona*)

Painted agamas (*Laudakia*)

Spiny-tailed agamids (*Uromastyx*)

Iguanids

Desert iguanas (*Dipsosaurus*)

Spiny-tailed iguanas (*Ctenosaura*)

Collared lizards (*Crotaphytus*)

Leopard lizards *(Gambelia)*
Fringe-footed lizards *(Uma)*
Chuckwallas *(Sauromalus)*
Utas *(Uta)*
Spiny lizards *(Sceloporus)*
Whiptail lizards *(Cnemidophorus)*

Lacertids

Many types of lacertas fare well in desert vivaria. The smaller species are recommended the most because they seldom dig up or damage plants.

Scincids

Barrel skinks *(Chalcides ocellatus)*
Schneider's skinks *(Eumeces schneideri)*
Sand skinks *(Scincus)*

Snakes

The following are some of the more readily available snakes that have proven successful in naturalistic desert vivaria. Avoid using ultra fine silica sands with these species; use natural desert sands or decomposed granite sands instead. You should create natural looking shelters. If you use rocks to create shelters, you should adhere them together with silicone cement or hot glue. With larger species of snakes, you should use only larger plants,as smaller plants will be crushed and damaged.

Boas and Pythons

Children's pythons *(Antaresia childreni)*
Spotted pythons *(Antaresia maculosa)*
Sand boas *(Eryx)*, all species
Rosy boas *(Lichanura)*, all species

Miniature Snakes

Ground snakes *(Sonora)*
Shovel-nosed snakes *(Chionactis)*

Colubrids

Glossy snakes *(Arizona)*
Desert, semiarid forms of common kingsnakes *(Lampropeltis getula californiensis, Lampropeltis g. splendida, Lampropeltis getula nitida)*
Arizona and Tarahumara mountain kingsnakes *(Lampropeltis pyromelana)*

Gray-banded kingsnakes *(Lampropeltis alterna)*
Trans-Pecos ratsnakes *(Dogertrophis subocularis)*
Green ratsnakes *(Senticolis triaspis)*
Baird's ratsnakes *(Elaphe bairdi)*
Egyptian diademe rat snakes *(Sphalaerosophis diadema)*
Black-headed diademe rat snakes *(Sphalaerosophis d. atriceps)*

Tortoises

Smaller species of tortoises can be kept in large desert vivaria; juveniles of some of the larger tortoises can be tried on a very short-term basis. Remember: tortoises are messy; vivaria with tortoises require regular cleaning if they are to remain attractive. As a rule, tortoises also are destructive to plant and landscape structures and are best kept in naturalistic vivaria which are large enough that bushes and large plants can be grown. Suitable species include some of the dwarf tortoises, such as *Testudo kleinmanni* and *Homopus signatus*. In very large vivaria, pancake tortoises and some of the Mediterranean tortoises will fare well.

All animals should be quarantined prior to introduction in a desert vivarium. They should be kept in simple setups with newspaper as a substrate unless they are a burrowing species. A paper substrate will allow you to monitor the feces. This imported frog-eyed gecko was regurgitating and had watery feces. It was treated for protozoan parasites and nematodes and has acclimated to captivity.

Keeping Mixed Collections in a Desert Vivarium

YOU CAN MIX various species of lizards in large desert vivaria, as long as you give care to selecting animals of more or less the same size that will inhabit different vivarium niches. For example, those geckos that dwell on rocks or walls will be compatible with many terrestrial species. Nocturnal geckos, which emerge at night, will be compatible with diurnal species of lizards of similar size. Remember the rules of animal density established at the beginning of this book [page 7].

Self-sustaining Vivaria

When working with miniature species or small species, it is sometimes possible to design self-sustaining vivaria in which animals will breed and increase in number without having to make special efforts or having to remove eggs for incubation. Self-sustaining vivaria are well suited to smaller gecko species. The author has had success with microgeckos *(Tropiocolotes)* in such setups. An area of the desert vivarium was regularly sprayed with water and the plants were watered regularly. These areas also served as egg-laying and-incubating sites. The author designed the vivarium to offer hiding places for the babies which, because of size, were not accessible to adults, thus allowing them to escape into these areas, if necessary. As long as sufficient food was available, the babies grew and essentially became part of the growing colony. This kind of approach could work well with many of the smaller geckos; you could start with a couple of pairs and gradually end up with many more. Of course, hypothetically there would come a point at which cannibalism, territorial behavior, or aggressive behavior would limit indefinite population expansion. For this reason, you would have to remove a certain number of pairs and introduce them to another similar setup, in order to keep the population expanding. Such setups can be very satisfying, allowing the observation of a wide range of behaviors and population dynamics that are not observable in other types of setups. Many gecko species will perform well under such conditions; so will small species of lacertas and possibly utas and various small skinks. Here again, there is much room for experimentation. The recommended ratio of vivarium length to animal length for a self-sustaining vivarium is at least 12 to one, meaning the vivarium length should be at least 12 times the total length of the largest animal to be maintained in that enclosure. It is therefore clear that, for most individuals, only smaller species of reptiles are suitable for experimental self-sustaining vivaria.

Arizona Mt. Kingsnake (Lampropeltis p. pyromelana). Photo by Jim Bridges and Bob Prince.

Vivarium Problems

Bᴇᴄᴀᴜsᴇ ᴛʜᴇʏ ᴄᴏᴍʙɪɴᴇ animals, substrate materials, and lights, vivaria can present a much greater range of challenges than those encountered when keeping amphibians and reptiles in simple setups. An obvious example involves the welfare of plants; vivarists can become as concerned about the condition of their plants as they do about their animals.

Ants

If the author were to name the most dreaded vivarium problem, it would be ants. These insects will attack crickets and mealworms and can kill baby lizards such as day geckos and baby chameleons. They are a nightmare in a naturalistic vivarium. If you find ants, you must tear apart the entire vivarium until you can locate their nest and remove it. The best way to avoid ant problems is prevention. Do *not* inadvertently introduce an ant colony along with plants or soil mixes. Check every soil mix thoroughly before introducing it into a vivarium; unpot and check root balls of any plant you are planning to use. Another way to help prevent ants is to methodically search out nests, both indoors and out, destroying them with ant traps, and spreading Sevin Dust® or carefully using ant spray in ant-infested areas.

Plant Pests

You can best prevent plant pests by carefully inspecting plants prior to introducing them into a vivarium. If you see pests, such as mealy bugs or aphids, take the plant out and proceed with treatment outside of the vivarium. Wait several weeks, then wash any residue of pesticides from the plant with dish detergent and water. After a thorough rinsing, you can reintroduce the plant into the vivarium.

Etiolation

When plants receive inadequate light to fulfill their requirements, they tend to grow lanky, stretched, weak, and deformed—a condition known as etiolation. This is a common problem with many cacti and succulents grown indoors. The solution is simple: increase the amount of available light. Herpetoculturists are now experimenting with metal halide and self-ballasted mercury vapor bulbs; these may prove very beneficial for desert vivaria. Besides emitting a generous amount of light and heat (both of which are desirable for desert plants and animals), these bulbs also generate relatively high ultraviolet (UV) levels. Some type of shield to protect humans from excessive UV exposure is required when using these bulbs. The amount of dietary vitamin D_3 offered animals should also be adjusted to reduce the risk of hypervitaminosis. Hopefully, more information on the use of these bulbs in herpetoculture will become available in the near future.

Plant Burns

When plants are exposed to excessive heat and light, they may burn. This will happen if you place plants directly under or too close to a spotlight.

Overwatering

If a desert vivarium has been overwatered, the wet substrate can become detrimental to both animals and plants. Arid plants typically rot if they are allowed to remain in a soggy substrate. To dry overwatered substrate out, roll newspaper into tight tubes and stick the ends into the substrate. Within 24 hours a fair amount of the excess water will be absorbed by the paper.

Soil Fungi

If a soil mix has not been sterilized properly, fungal mycelia may grow through the soil and may eventually produce mushrooms. In desert vivaria, such mushroom production rapidly becomes self-limiting, particularly if you allow the soil to dry out and if you quickly remove any mushrooms that appear. A more serious problem is fungi that attack the roots or stems of plants. These pests are best prevented by using an airy soil mix, using a subtank heater to keep the ground temperature moderately warm, and allowing a brief drying out of soil between waterings. You *cannot* use fungicides in desert vivaria. If a plant shows clear signs of fungal rot (for example, if a section of caudex is rotting), then remove the plant and treat it with a fungicide such as Benomyl®. Wait until several weeks of fungicide-free maintenance have passed before returning the plant to the vivarium. If you are in doubt about the plant's health or about fungicide residues, it is best to replace that plant with a new one.

This is a small sampling of the plants the author keeps in his garden for vivaria design.

The Vivarium as an Educational Tool

IN THE SUMMER of 1993, the AFH sponsored a graduate course *Herpetoculture in the Classroom* offered in Rock Springs, Wyoming through the Univerisity of Wyoming. This conference and workshop has had increasing success and has become a forum for conveying and exchanging ideas on some of the most up-to-date herpetocultural methods, including vivarium design. The author gave several lectures to the many teachers who attended, and it became clear that naturalistic vivaria have considerable value as educational tools.

Ideally, a well-designed vivarium is a type of open-system, manmade microcosm that contains many of the elements which characterize natural habitats. It presents numerous opportunities for the gathering of data and for an investigation of some of the important components of habitats, including microclimatic and topographical elements, as well as various aspects of animal behavior.

What Can be Learned About the Animals?

During a 24-hour period, animals commonly demonstrate definite patterns of activity. These patterns are carried out in select areas of any vivarium. If a vivarium has three shelters, each with a different temperature and a different relative humidity, which ones do the animals select and when? If a large group of a given species is kept together, the individual animals will segregate or congregate, spreading out in select areas of the vivarium. What are their patterns of behavior? Does a species avoid three-dimensional landscape structures or use them? Are there noticeable differences in behavior when you change the type of lighting used?

Reptiles in a naturalistic vivaria will also show definite defecation patterns that may not be observable in smaller enclosures. What are those patterns? What function could they possibly serve?

At night, by using red incandescent bulbs, the nocturnal behavior of reptiles can be observed. Behavior that one may never be able to observe otherwise is suddenly revealed, particularly in nocturnal speicies of geckos.

We are convinced that opportunities for learning are considerable when you keep amphibians and reptiles in naturalistic vivaria, particularly when you combine observation of the vivaria with literature research of geography, ecology, climatology, and animal behavior.

Conclusion

IT IS HOPED that the basic principles of desert vivarium design have been presented successfully in this relatively short book, although the entire field of naturalistic vivarium design is still in its infancy. What we know today will undoubtedly pale in light of all that lies ahead.

I am particularly excited about the potential role of naturalistic vivaria in education, not only in schools but also in the home environment. Naturalistic vivaria present unique opportunities for young people and adults to observe events that are not the standard course in the life of urbanized, technologically oriented humans. When they are well designed, vivaria become windows into some of the complexity of the natural world. To observe and grasp complex relationships can only expand human consciousness and help reveal the depth of the world in which we live. Furthermore, I am convinced that exposure to, and above all caring for, animals and plants will help our children become adults with dimensionality and heart.

Taking the time to learn and develop the right vivarium environment for your animals will give the animals the quality of life that will allow for successful natural reproduction opportunities.

Useful Sources of Information

De Vosjoli, P. 1994. The Lizard Keeper's Handbook. Advanced Vivarium Systems, Santee, CA. Essential information for successfully keeping lizards in captivity.

Zimmerman, E. 1986. Breeding Terrarium Animals. T.F.H. A good basic book on herpetoculture and vivarium design.

For information on high quality vivarium enclosures write to: Vivarium Research Group, Inc., Cold Blooded® Vivaria, PO Box 5640, Lighthouse Point, Florida 33074. Tel# (954) 984-0009 Fax# (954) 984-0012.

Books on plants

Chahinian, B.J.1986. The Sansevieria Trifasciata Varieties: A presentation of all cultivated varieties. Trans Terra Publishing, Reseda, CA. All cultivars of S. trifasciata are presented in color along with good basic information.

Graf, A.B. 1981. Tropica: Color Cyclopedia of Exotic Plants and Trees. Roehrs Company. East Rutherford N.J. 07073. The classic horticultural reference work. Expensive but an essential reference for the serious vivarist.

Stover, H . 1983. The Sansevieria Book. Endangered Species P.O. Box Tustin Ca 92681. This book has 75 black and white photos and all the basic information on this neat group of plants you need to know. Endangered species also has a catalog that offers the most extensive selection of snakeplants anywhere.

Organizations

American Federation of Herpetoculturists
P.O. Box 300067
Escondido, CA 92030-0067
Membership: $26.00
This organization publishes *The Vivarium*, a high quality magazine at the cutting edge of herpetoculture.

Cactus and Succulent Society of America
P.O. Box 35034HP
Des Moines Iowa 50315-0301
Membership: $30.00
A great source of information on cultivating plants suitable for desert vivaria. Their publications also have numerous mail-order sources for plants.

Index

A
Agamids 56
Ants 59

B
Basking areas 17
Boas and pythons 57
Books 63

C
Colubrids 57
Complex-Naturalistic vivarium
 approach 15
Cubed vivarium 21

D
Drainage layer 16

E
Enclosure
  commercial 9
  custom-made 10
  front-opening 11
  selection 9
Equipment 53
Etiolation 46, 59

F
Food 55

G
Geckos 56

H
Heat distribution 52
Heat controls 54
Heaters 52

Hot-rock 52
Hygrometers 53

I
Iguanids 56
Information 63

L
Lacertids 57

N
Naturalistic vivarium 6

O
Organizations 63

P
Plant
  burns 59
    maintenance 47
    overview 26-27, 45-46
    pests 59
    placement 24
    rot 46
    sources of 23
    watering 46, 59

R
Rocks 19

S
Sand 13
Scincids 57
Shelters 22
Snakes
  miniature 57

Stands 10
Submerged-pot approach 13
Substrates 16
  drainage layer 16
  growing medium 17
  surface medium 17
Sunken-Pipe approach 15
Sunken-Pot approach 13
Soil 60

T
Timers 51
Topographical stratification 6
Tortoises 57
Thermostats 54

V
Vivarist 6
Vivarium
  cubed vivarium 21
  design 12, 18, 21, 47
  educational tool 61
  landscaping 17
  maturation 48
  self-sustaining 58
Vivarium Store
  requirements 5
  specialized 4

W
Watering 46, 59
Winter dormancy 47
Wood 22